christian

Christian Morality
In the Breath of God

Catholic Basics
A Pastoral Ministry Series

Russell B. Connors Jr.

Thomas P. Walters, Ph.D.
Series Editor

NATIONAL CONFERENCE FOR
CATECHETAL LEADERSHIP

LOYOLAPRESS.
3441 N. ASHLAND AVENUE
CHICAGO, ILLINOIS 60657

NIHIL OBSTAT: Rev. Daniel J. Mahan, S.T.B., S.T.L.
                      Censor Librorum

IMPRIMATUR: Rev. Msgr. Joseph F. Schaedel
                      Vicar General/Moderator of the Curia

Given at Indianapolis, Indiana, on February 19, 2001

The *nihil obstat* and *imprimatur* are official declarations that a book is free of doctrinal and moral error. No implication is contained herein that those who have granted the *nihil obstat* and *imprimatur* agree with the content, opinions, or statements expressed.

Acknowledgments appearing on page 110 constitute a continuatuion of the copyright page.

Cover Design: Other Brother Design
Cover Illustration: Steve Snodgrass
Interior Illustrations: Other Brother Design

Library of Congress Cataloging-in-Publication Data

Connors, Russell B., 1948–
    Christian morality : in the breath of God / Russell B. Connors, Jr.
      p. cm. – (Catholic basics)
    Includes bibliographical references.
    ISBN 0-8294-1722-2
    1. Christian ethics–Catholic authorss. II. Title. III. Series.

BJ1249 .C475 2001
241'.042–dc21   2001029643
                                                                                                  CIP

ISBN: 0-8294-1722-2

Published by Loyola Press, 3441 N. Ashland Avenue, Chicago, Illinois 60657 U.S.A.
© 2002 The National Conference for Catechetical Leadership.

01   02   03   04   05   Bang   5   4   3   2   1

Table of Contents

About the Series   viii

Certification Standards: National Resources for
    Church Ministry   ix

Preface   xi

Introduction   xii

CHAPTER 1: **Christian Morality and the**
Love of God   1
From the *Catechism*   2
Christian Moral Life as Response to the Love of God   3
Christian Moral Life as Life in the Spirit   7
Christian Moral Life as Sacramental Life   10
For Reflection   13
For Further Reading   13

CHAPTER 2: **Christian Morality and the**
Reign of God   15
From the *Catechism*   16
Christian Convictions About the Reign of God   18
Christian Moral Life as Active Participation in Christ's
    Work of Building the Reign of God   20
Christian Moral Life and "Thisworldliness"   24
For Reflection   27
For Further Reading   27

CHAPTER 3: **Christian Morality and the**
Process of Conscience   28
From the *Catechism*   29
Conscience as Capacity for Goodness and Rightness   31
Conscience as Process: The Homework of Moral
    Decision Making   33

Conscience as Judgment: Taking Responsibility 38
For Reflection 41
For Further Reading 41

CHAPTER 4: **CHRISTIAN MORALITY AND THE DYNAMICS OF SIN AND CONVERSION** 43
From the *Catechism* 44
Sin: "Original" and "Actual" 45
Conversion as Command and Possibility 50
Resurrection Faith and Christian Hope 53
For Reflection 56
For Further Reading 56

CHAPTER 5: **CHRISTIAN MORALITY AND ISSUES OF HEALTH AND LIFE** 58
From the *Catechism* 59
Catholic Convictions Concerning the Promotion of Health and the Preservation of Life 60
Catholic Convictions Concerning Direct and "Indirect" Killing 63
Catholic Convictions Concerning the Use and Nonuse of Medical Treatment 67
For Reflection 70
For Further Reading 71

CHAPTER 6: **CHRISTIAN MORALITY AND HUMAN SEXUALITY** 72
From the *Catechism* 74
Christian Faith and Sexuality: Creation and Integration 75
Norms and Values: Specific Issues 79
"Laws of Growth" 84
For Reflection 86
For Further Reading 87

CHAPTER 7: **CHRiStiaп MORaLitY aпD SOCiaL ReSpoпSibiLitY** 89

From the *Catechism* 91

Starting Points: Human Dignity and Human Rights 92

Focus: Economic Justice 97

"Preferential Love for the Poor" 101

For Reflection 105

For Further Reading 106

Conclusion 107

Bibliography 109

Acknowledgments 110

About the Author 111

About the Series

Catholic Basics: A Pastoral Ministry Series offers an in-depth yet accessible understanding of the fundamentals of the Catholic faith for adults, both those preparing for lay ministry and those interested in the topics for their own personal growth. The series helps readers explore the Catholic tradition and apply what they have learned to their lives and ministry situations. Each title offers a reliable introduction to a specific topic and provides a foundational understanding of the concepts.

Each book in the series presents a Catholic understanding of its topic as found in Scripture and the teachings of the Church. Each of the authors has paid special attention to the documents of the Second Vatican Council and the *Catechism of the Catholic Church*, so that further learning can be guided by these core resources.

Chapters conclude with study questions that may be used for small group review or for individual reflection. Additionally, suggestions for further reading offer dependable guides for extra study.

The initiative of the National Conference of Catechetical Leadership led to the development of an earlier version of this series. The indispensable contribution of the series editor, Dr. Thomas Walters, helped ensure that the concepts and ideas presented here are easily accessible to a wide audience.

CERTIFICATION STANDARDS: NATIONAL RESOURCES FOR CHURCH MINISTRY

E ach book in this theology series relates to standards for theological competency identified in the resources listed below. Three national church ministry organizations provide standards for certification programs that serve their respective ministries. The standards were developed in collaboration with the United States Catholic Conference Commission on Certification and Accreditation. The fourth resource is the latest document, developed to identify common goals of the three sets of standards.

Competency Based Certification Standards for Pastoral Ministers, Pastoral Associates and Parish Life Coordinators. Chicago: National Association for Lay Ministry, Inc. (NALM), 1994.

These standards address three roles found in pastoral ministry settings in the United States. They were the earliest to receive approval from the United States Catholic Conference Commission on Certification and Accreditation. Copies are available from the National Association for Lay Ministry, 5420 S. Cornell, Chicago, IL 60615-5604.

National Certification Standards for Professional Parish Directors of Religious Education. Washington, DC: National Conference for Catechetical Leadership, 1998.

NCCL developed standards to foster appropriate initial education and formation, as well as continuing personal and professional development, of those who serve as directors of religious education (DREs). The standards address various areas of knowledge and abilities needed in the personal, theological, and professional aspects of the ministry. Also included is a code of ethics for professional catechetical leaders. Available from the National Conference of Catechetical Leadership, 3021 Fourth Street NE, Washington, DC 20017-1102.

NFCYM Competency-Based Standards for the Coordinator of Youth Ministry. Washington, DC: National Federation for Catholic Youth Ministry, 1996.

This document lays out the wide range of knowledge and skills that support ministry with young people, as well as the successful leadership and organization of youth ministry wherever it may be situated. The standards are available from the National Federation for Catholic Youth Ministry, 415 Michigan Avenue NE, Suite 40, Washington, DC 20017-1518.

Merkt, Joseph T., ed. *Common Formation Goals for Ministry*. A joint publication of NALM, NFCYM, and NCCL, 2000.

Rev. Joseph Merkt compared the documentation of standards cited by three national organizations serving pastoral, youth, and catechetical ministries. The resulting statement of common goals identifies common ground for those who prepare persons for ministry, as well as for the many who wear multiple hats. Copies are available from NALM, NCCL, or NFCYM.

PREFACE

Several acknowledgments are in order. First, I am grateful to Bishop Anthony Pilla, from the Diocese of Cleveland, Ohio, and to a group of colleagues at St. Mary Seminary in Cleveland for providing the invitation and the setting to study the *Catechism of the Catholic Church* when it was first published several years ago. Those conversations—which led to a series of articles on the Catechism by Bishop Pilla—continued to nourish me with ideas and insights as I wrote. I am indebted to Amy Clancy and to Rita Chilar from the Theology Department at the College of St. Catherine where I currently teach. Their proofreading was helpful as was Rita's "technical assistance" (helping me figure out some of the mysteries of my computer). My thanks also goes to my wife, Patty, not only for her proofreading of the text, but for listening to me talk through so many of my ideas—especially over breakfast. This book is better (as am I) because of the way she listens and because of the way she speaks up.

Introduction

Years ago, when I was just starting to study moral theology, a friend of mine used to enjoy teasing me about the nature of my discipline. His area of graduate studies was Christian faith itself. So when we were at social gatherings and people would ask what he studied, he'd reply, "I focus on God—God's love, God's grace, God's Spirit." Then the question would turn to me, but before I could explain what I studied, my friend would jump in and say, "Oh, he does moral theology—you know, all the rules and regulations of Catholicism. It's the dark side of the Good News; somebody's got to do it."

"The dark side of the Good News." If this book has one main purpose, I suppose it could be said that its aim is to prove my friend wrong. Christian morality is nothing other than living in Christ—living in the love, grace, and Spirit of Christ, the Spirit of God.

Is it difficult to follow Christ? Is it a challenge to be faithful to the Gospel? Can it be exhausting to devote oneself to building up God's reign of love and justice on this earth? Of course! But that is a far cry from "the dark side of the Good News." Whatever else it involves, the Christian moral life begins with the experience that we are loved by God in an unimaginable, unfathomable way. The Christian moral life is our attempt to respond to the gift of that love. The primary aim of this book is to convey that conviction as we look at some of the important themes and dimensions of Christian morality.

I have tried to write in a nontechnical, reader-friendly style, inviting readers to reflect along the way on their own experience as Christian moral persons. Although each of the seven chapters should be able to "stand on its own two feet," there is an overall rationale for the book's outline. The first two chapters are companions. With different emphases, they attempt to answer the question, "Just what is Christian morality?" Chapter 1 emphasizes God. Christian moral living is about responding to God's love, so we first reflect on the nature of that love. The emphasis of chapter 2 is on ourselves. Christian morality concerns our call to take an active role in the work of the reign of God.

Chapter 3 focuses on the reality of conscience. I propose a threefold way of looking at conscience that turns out to be something of a model for decision making for Christian people. Chapter 4 turns its attention to what might be called the "dynamics" of Christian living. We look at the nature of sin and its power in our lives and in the world. But more importantly (because if sin abounds, grace abounds more), we discuss resurrection faith and Christian hope and how they impact the human processes of conversion. I think this chapter is filled with very good news.

The last three chapters focus on specific areas of Christian moral responsibility. Chapter 5 is an overview of some important Catholic convictions about the promotion of our health and the preservation of human life. It is a quick excursion into medical ethics from a Catholic perspective. Chapter 6 addresses some important themes and ideas concerning human sexuality, chief among them being the goodness and sacredness of sexuality and our call to live our lives sexually, not only with joy and delight but also with honesty and responsibility. Chapter 7 presents some of the key convictions of Catholic social teaching, with emphasis on human dignity, human rights (especially economic rights), and what the *Catechism of the Catholic Church (CCC)* calls "a preferential love for the poor."

The primary source for this book is the *CCC*. Readers would do well to have a copy of the *Catechism* nearby. Sometimes I will quote the text of the *Catechism*, but at other times I will simply refer to paragraph numbers from the text. At the same time, much of what is presented here is consonant with the ideas and insights of a number of contemporary Catholic theologians. To be clear, the aim is not to provide a detailed commentary on all the sections of the *CCC* that have something to do with morality, but rather to present an overview of the Christian moral life, drawing regularly from material in the *CCC*. If this book sheds light on what it means for you to respond to the love of God, and if it helps you understand the connection between that response and some of the concrete moral challenges of your life, my efforts will have been worthwhile.

CHAPTER 1

Christian Morality and the Love of God

ᛗIKE

I t's wonderful to talk to Mike these days. On the one hand, he's the same old Mike—an opinionated, strong-willed, confirmed bachelor whose bark, as everyone has always known, is a lot more ferocious than his bite. On the other hand, there is something delightfully new about Mike. You see, he has fallen in love. That's the only way to put it. There is a joy about him now that starts deep down inside and bubbles up spontaneously to the surface as you listen to him talk. As you might guess, Mike struggles to put into words just what he's experiencing. At one of his more articulate moments he put it this way: "Heck, I was happy before, but not like this. I don't really know where Maria came from or how she found her way into my life, but I think I'm going to spend the rest of my life being thankful and trying to respond to the gift that she is."

From the *Catechism:* Paragraph 1692

Perhaps it seems odd, but there is a connection between Mike's experience and what the Christian moral life and this book are all about.

Mike has been "knocked off his feet" by Maria. In his words, she is a "gift," and he has an inkling that he is going to spend the rest of his life not only being grateful, but trying to respond to the awesome gift that Maria's love—that Maria herself—is for him.

What is the Christian moral life? It is nothing other than the recognition of the amazing gift of God's loving presence in our lives and our continuing effort to respond to that love. That's it. Living our lives as Christians may not always be easy (that's an understatement), but it does not seem complicated. God loves us amazingly, especially in and through the person and work of Jesus Christ. Christians are those who know this and who spend their lives being thankful and trying to respond to the gift of God's love. May none of the pages and ideas that follow come to obscure or interfere with this simple but profound understanding of what the Christian life is all about.

If Christian living is a matter of responding to God's love, then it seems important to reflect on that love and what it means to respond to it. That is the first order of business of this chapter. After that I connect this with the Spirit of God and propose that Christian living means living in the Spirit. The chapter concludes with a more specific reflection on Christian sacramental life, with special attention to Baptism and Eucharist.

Christian Moral Life as Response to the Love of God

If the Christian moral life, in an overarching way, can be described as a life of response to God's love, then it is important to begin by noting some things about that love. So what shall we say about God and the love of God? That is even more difficult than asking Mike to describe Maria; words will fall short. Nevertheless, I propose that there are three things that should command our attention.

First, it is important to remind ourselves of a core Christian conviction: God is love. This is not simply a repetition of a couple of verses from the First Letter of John in the New Testament (see 1 John 4:8 and 16), but an overriding conviction of both the Old Testament and the New Testament. The Israelites seemed to believe, for example, that God's saving action on their behalf—in rescuing them from slavery in Egypt and helping them begin their journey toward their own land—revealed something not only about what God could do, but about who God was: an amazing and gracious God of love. And over and over in the parables of Jesus—most notably in Luke's story of the prodigal son (see 15:11–32), perhaps more properly called the story of the loving father—it is not something that is revealed to us, but someone: God, whose love is so all-encompassing that it is appropriate to say that God *is* love.

This should not strike us as something completely foreign. An analogy with human love is helpful here. Mike, for example, knows that he has received an amazing gift. He has not received something *from* Maria; he has received Maria herself. That is what genuine love is about, is it not? It is the gift of self to another. When we love another, we give the gift of ourselves—our minds and hearts, time and talents, hopes and concerns. The more totally we love, the more complete is the gift. This is not to say that we who have experienced the gift of God's presence and love in our lives have received "all there is" of God. God is also mystery. To use a spatial image that falls far short of the reality, God is "bigger" than our minds and hearts can receive fully. And yet what we know of God is real. What we believe is that God loves us in a way that reveals not simply what God does, but who God is.

A second dimension of God's love to which we should give some attention is prompted by a question: "How does God love us?" Now there are probably a hundred good answers to that question. But here is one that seems close to the core of Christian faith: God loves us graciously. The author of the New Testament Letter to the Ephesians expressed well what the graciousness of God's love is all about.

> But God, who is rich in mercy, out of great love with which he loved us even when we were dead through our trespasses, made us alive together with Christ—by grace you have been saved—and raised us up with him and seated us with him in the heavenly places in Christ Jesus, so that in the ages to come he might show the immeasurable riches of his grace in kindness toward us in Christ Jesus. For by grace you have been saved through faith, and this is not your own doing; it is the gift of God—not the result of works, so that no one may boast.
>
> (2:4–9)

This passage captures an important Christian conviction. God loves us not because our good deeds have earned that love and not because we always do the right thing—because, as we all know, we don't. No, God's love is given to us independent of our goodness or badness, rightness or wrongness. The word in Christian tradition for this is *grace*; God's love is given freely, just because that is the way God is.

The parables of Jesus point to this truth often. In the story of the loving father, for example, the celebration that was held upon the prodigal son's return was obviously not in response to his fidelity, or even because this son was moved with remorse (more than anything else, it seems, he returned because he was hungry). The father was rich in mercy, lavish in love. That is the point. That is God's way, God's gracious way of loving.

A third aspect of God's love that calls for our attention is the fact that God's love is powerful; it is transformative. The all-important exodus event for the Israelites displays this well. God was revealed in the Israelites' midst as a God who cared about their plight. But God's love and care involved more than a feeling. And so we read in the story:

> I have observed the misery of my people who are in Egypt; I have heard their cry on account of their taskmasters. Indeed, I know their sufferings, and I have come down to deliver them from the Egyptians, and to bring them up out of that land to a good and broad land.
>
> (Exodus 3:7–8)

This great story reveals well the nature of God's love; it is a verb. God's love is made manifest in powerful deeds—deeds of compassion, healing, and justice. Just as Mike seems to be "a new person" because of the way Maria's love has touched him, so too (but even more) those who are touched by the powerful love of God are made new. The story of "the good thief" who hung on a cross next to Jesus on Calvary displays this truth dramatically. In that story, the forgiving love of God was revealed through the words and deeds of Jesus, and in a simple but profound way, the thief was forgiven (see Luke 23:39–43). God's love makes us new.

So what are the implications of all of this? We are saying that God is love, that God loves us all freely and graciously, and that

God's love is made manifest in powerful, transformative deeds. And how does this information bear on Christian living? The answer to that question seems to be captured well in this brief passage from the First Letter of John from the New Testament.

> *God's love was revealed among us in this way: God sent his only Son into the world so that we might live through him. In this is love, not that we loved God but that he loved us and sent his Son to be the atoning sacrifice for our sins. Beloved, since God loved us so much, we also ought to love one another. No one has ever seen God; if we love one another, God lives in us, and his love is perfected in us.*
>
> (4:9–12)

Christian living, the author tells us, begins with an appreciation of the gift of God's life and love in our midst, the gift of Jesus Christ. But it does not stop there; rather, it moves to a response that is nothing less than loving one another with the same love that we have received. Note that the passage does not simply say that we are to imitate the love of God (the self-giving, gracious, transformative love of God). No, we are to love with the same love with which God loves us. When we love in self-giving, gracious, and transformative ways, this passage would have us believe, then God is "dwelling" in us, God is at work in us, and somehow God's presence in the world is brought to greater perfection through us.

Can we take this seriously? Do we really think we can love in this way? Do passages like this, which suggest that we should be holy as God is holy (see Leviticus 19:2) or that we should be compassionate as God is compassionate (see Colossians 3:12–13) push us to be "spiritual overachievers"—and leave us feeling like ultimate failures? Are we capable of loving and living this way? To answer these questions, let us look to other key ingredients of our faith: our convictions about the Spirit of God.

Christian Moral Life as Life in the Spirit

I would hardly be the first to suggest that over the centuries (and into our day) the Holy Spirit has tended to be the forgotten one of the Christian Trinity of Father-Son-Spirit. There may be many reasons for this, perhaps not least among them being the fact that images for this third "member" of the Trinity—wind, fire, etc.—are so elusive. Perhaps the authors of the *Catechism of the Catholic Church (CCC)* hoped to correct this. Perhaps that is why the very first chapter of the first section of part 3—the part that deals most directly with Christian morality—is entitled "Man's Vocation: Life in the Spirit." Taking this cue from the *CCC*, let us reflect briefly—and in a threefold way—on what it means to say that our vocation is to live in the Spirit of God.

Staying in close contact with the text of the *CCC*, the first thing to note about our call to live in the Spirit relates to Christian faith concerning our creation. The *CCC* tells us that the dignity we have as persons is based on the fact that we have been created in the image of God (see #1700), that God's image is present in all of us (see #1702), and that because of this wonderful way we have been created we participate in the light and power of the Spirit of God (see #1704).

Taking these texts seriously leads to startling conclusions. For instance, if I truly believe that I am made in the image of God, that I participate in the light and power of the divine Spirit, then at my darkest hour of failure or sinfulness, I am called to believe that I am still holy. I am called to believe, as the poster suggests, that "God did not make junk" when God created me. And if I were to take seriously that everyone is created in God's Spirit and is, therefore, a "dwelling place" of God's living presence, then indeed I would care if there were even one person anywhere on this earth who was hungry or poor or abandoned or abused—much less millions of people! And if I were a Catholic in Northern Ireland and had grown up in a culture of suspicion and hatred for Protestants, or if I were a Christian in Jerusalem living in near despair over the centuries-old religiously motivated hostilities in the Middle East, or if I were a black woman in the Deep

South in 1850 and had grown up with the indignity and abuses of slavery and wondered if there could ever be freedom and common decency for all people, then the belief in the presence of the Holy Spirit in every human being—regardless of age, race, gender, ethnic background, economic status, or any other potentially divisive factor—might give me reason for hope and motivation to work for justice and peace. That is the point—or at least part of the point. If all human beings have the Spirit of the living God within them, then everyone is holy and should be treated not only with respect but also with reverence! That, I think, is what the *CCC* would have us believe.

A second important feature of what "life in the Spirit" means has to do with our connection with Jesus Christ himself. To live a Christian life is not simply to live like Christ, or to try to imitate Christ, for in the end, on our own power, we will fall short. Rather, Christian life begins with the belief that in some amazing and transforming way, Christ lives in us. There is a power, a life, in us that is not simply our own; this power, this life, is God's power, God's life, and, more specifically, it is the power of the Spirit of God.

This means at least two things. First, we are called and empowered to continue the mission and ministry of Jesus Christ in our world today. It is the Spirit of God who makes that possible. Our faith invites us to believe that as we receive the gift of the Holy Spirit we are at the same time receiving the Spirit of Jesus Christ. And if Jesus' mission and ministry on this earth were all about reconciliation, healing, forgiveness, and love (among other things), then our lives must "be about" the same things. It is the Spirit of God that "connects us" with the mission and ministry of Jesus.

Second, we should notice that the Spirit of God that is shared with us and that connects us with Christ is the Spirit of the risen Christ, victorious over death. One passage from John's Gospel that the *CCC* refers to in particular (see John 19:28–30) does not present a picture of Jesus handing over his spirit in a moment of defeat, but in a moment of victory. We receive the Spirit of God from Jesus who was victorious over the powers of trial and temptation, sickness and suffering, damnation and death.

None of this is to say, of course, that Christian life—life in the Spirit—is easy. But it is to say that living like Christ and in his Spirit means living with a kind of power and a source of hope that would otherwise be impossible. If temptation, suffering, and death did not have the last word in the life of Jesus, they will not have the last word for those who live in his Spirit either.

A third and final feature of what "life in the Spirit" means deals with living in love. And in a sense this brings us around "full circle" to where we began: Christian living is living in the love of God. Recalling two New Testament passages, the *CCC* puts it this way:

> "God is Love" (1 John 4:8 and 16), and love is his first gift, containing all others. "God's love has been poured into our hearts through the Holy Spirit who has been given to us" (Romans 5:5).
>
> (#733)

It is through the power of the Holy Spirit, this passage instructs, that the love of God has been given to us. And further, the gift of God's love in us is a living and abiding gift.

The closest analogy we have for this—one that may make these reflections less "dizzying"—is the gift of human love. Mike senses that the gift of Maria's love is not a momentary or passing gift, but one that is enduring. In a sense, he has received Maria herself in a mysterious, wonderful, and abiding way. And it looks as though Mike is gearing up to base the rest of his life on that gift. All the more so with God. Our Christian faith invites us to believe that through the power of the Spirit we have received nothing less than the gift of God into our lives in an enduring, abiding way. Our faith invites us also to live our lives in response to that love by doing what we can to love others as God has loved us. It is the Spirit of God who makes this possible.

Christian Moral Life as Sacramental Life

If the thesis of this chapter is that the Christian moral life is, at its core, a life of response to God's love, this conviction is dramatized in a magnificent way in the celebration of the sacraments. Let us examine this briefly with regard to the sacraments of Baptism and Eucharist.

BAPTISM

The *CCC* discusses the importance of Baptism at some length, but for our purposes three things about this sacrament seem particularly significant: Baptism is about dying and rising; it is about access to a special kind of grace and power; and it is about incorporation into the Body of Christ.

Commenting on the origins of the word *baptism*, the *CCC* explains that when we are "plunged" into the water we are "plunged" into Christ's death, so that we can rise with him as new creatures (see #1214).

There can be no mistake about it; as this text reminds us, to be initiated into Christ means entering into an ongoing process of dying and rising. Most dramatically at the Easter Vigil Liturgy, when the catechumens are plunged into the baptismal water, it is dramatized for the entire community what it means to live as followers of Jesus. We must be buried with Christ so that we can be raised up with Christ. We must be willing to die to selfishness and sin so that we can live lives of selflessness and grace. Note that Baptism is a one-time event; it is not repeated. At the same time, however, baptismal life is a never-ending process, a process of letting go of what is old about us so that we can be renewed in God's love and grace.

Later on in its treatment of Baptism, the *CCC* comments on the grace of Baptism. What the grace of this sacrament enables the baptized to do is: "to live and act under the prompting of the Holy Spirit . . . allowing them to grow in goodness through moral virtues" (#1266).

This is an important and insightful text. It makes clear that the presence and power of the Holy Spirit, received in a new way in Baptism, are given to us so that we may live and act in Spirit-guided ways and thereby grow in goodness and virtue. We will look at this more closely in our discussion of conscience and decision making in chapter 3. For now we should note simply that for Christians, the presence of God's Spirit in our lives should change the question we ask ourselves as we consider difficult moral choices. For the believer, the question "What do I think I should do?" might become "What do I believe the Spirit of God is prompting me to do?" As we shall see, those questions need not be in conflict, but the latter question opens us up to a source of wisdom not accessible to those who ask only the first question.

Finally, it is through Baptism that we become part of the Body of Christ. Two things are important about this. First, the Christian life is not lived alone. To use directional images, our life of response to the love of God is not simply a vertical, God-and-I, Jesus-and-I, affair. The Christian life has a horizontal dimension: it concerns our relationships with one another. This is important not simply because we are called to demonstrate our love of God through our love of neighbor, but—just as important—because we actually encounter the presence of God in our neighbor (see Matthew 25:31–46, for example). Together we are the Body of Christ in this world. We come to know and love Christ through coming to know and love one another.

The second thing to notice about the passage above is that incorporation into the Body of Christ is an invitation—a challenge—to recognize our essential unity with one another, a unity that is meant to overcome any of the divisions of nationality, culture, race, or gender. This is both a present reality and a future hope. It is real because one need only look around to notice the amazing diversity that exists among the followers of Christ. It is nothing short of a miracle that there is enough "glue" to hold us together. That "glue," of course, is the Spirit of God! But it is also true that we are not quite the Body of Christ that we are called to be; we are also a sinful people. The history of Christianity bears the marks of far too many factions and divisions that continue to be part of who we are today. So together we long for the day when God's Spirit will bring our unity to completion.

One could say a thousand things about the importance of the Eucharist for the Christian life. Recalling the teaching of the Second Vatican Council, the *CCC* reminds us that the Eucharist is "the source and summit of the Christian life" (#1324, *LG* 11). At this point let us add only two further comments.

First, the Eucharist is fundamentally about thanksgiving. In this sacrament, we express our gratitude for everything that God has done for us, especially through the love of Jesus Christ (see #1360).

This chapter emphasizes that the Christian moral life is essentially a life of response to the love of God—and central to that, of course, is thanksgiving. To return to the story at the beginning of the chapter, Mike is amazingly grateful for the gift of Maria's love. Hopefully, that will stay with him forever. So, too, Christians are those who have experienced the gift of God's love in their life. Their first and most basic response is to be grateful. Nowhere is this "posture of thanksgiving" dramatized better than in the Eucharist.

Second, as the *CCC* reminds us, the eucharistic liturgy ends with our being sent into the world to extend the mission and ministry of Christ to those we meet in our daily lives (see #1332). Among many other things, the Eucharist is food for the journey. It is for those who know that responding to God's love in their daily lives is not easy. It is for those who know the world's wounds and their own limitations as they try to be followers of Christ on a day-to-day basis. Eucharist is not a reward for those who have arrived, but nourishment for those who are on the way.

For Reflection

1. This chapter opens with an analogy: our attempt to respond to the gift of God's love is like our attempt to respond to the gift of human love. In what way does this analogy seem to work? No doubt it is true that all analogies (certainly those we use in reference to God) fall short. How does this analogy fall short?

2. The chapter notes three things about the love of God: God is love; God's love is gracious; God's love is powerful. Which of these aspects of God's love is most striking to you? Why? Drawing on your own experience, what else would you like to say about God's love?

3. The chapter names several implications of saying that the Spirit of God dwells in all people. What were they? What do you think of them? What other implications can you think of for the conviction that God is "discoverable" in all people?

4. The chapter concludes with some reflections on the relationship between Baptism and the Eucharist in the Christian moral life. Drawing on your own experience of these sacraments, how would you describe the connection between these sacraments and the way we live our lives as Christians?

For Further Reading

Connors, Russell B. Jr., and Patrick T. McCormick. *Character, Choices and Community: The Three Faces of Christian Ethics*. Mahwah, NJ: Paulist Press, 1998.

The First Letter of John from the New Testament.

Hill, Brennan, and William Madges. *The Catechism: Highlights and Commentary*. Mystic, CT: Twenty-Third Publications, 1994.

O'Keefe, Mark, O.S.B. *Becoming Good, Becoming Holy: On the Relationship of Christian Ethics and Spirituality*. Mahwah, NJ: Paulist Press, 1995.

Second Vatican Council. "The Call to Holiness." Chap. 8 in *Lumen Gentium (Dogmatic Constitution on the Church)*, 1964.

Wadell, Paul. *The Primacy of Love: An Introduction to the Ethics of Thomas Aquinas*. Mahwah, NJ: Paulist Press, 1992.

CHAPTER 2

Christian Morality and the Reign of God

MR. PIAZZA

Once upon a time there was a garden, and the gardener was Mr. Piazza. It was the best garden in the village. Mrs. Farinacci was particularly fond of the garden. On her afternoon walks, when she would come upon Mr. Piazza tending the garden, she would usually remark, "Why Mr. Piazza, you and God have the most beautiful garden in the village." "Well, thank you," Mr. Piazza would reply.

This went on for some time. Then one hot and humid afternoon, Mr. Piazza was laboring hard in the garden, wiping the sweat from his brow as he worked. As was her habit, Mrs. Farinacci came along and remarked, "Mr. Piazza, I tell you, you and God have the most magnificent garden in all the village." This time Mr. Piazza stopped what he was doing, took off his hat, wiped the sweat from his brow, looked Mrs. Farinacci squarely in the eye, and said, "With all due respect, let me tell you something, my dear lady. This may be a magnificent garden, but as for me and God having it together, well, you should have seen the mess this garden was in when God had it all by himself!"

From the *Catechism:* Paragraphs 668, 669, 670, 671, 672

Surely Mr. Piazza in our opening story does not seem ready to deny that God has a role to play in what happens in his garden, but just as surely, he is intent on letting Mrs. Farinacci know that the blossoming of the flowers has a good deal to do with his own sweat in the heat of the day.

This chapter is about the relationship between what God is doing in this world and what we are called to do with him. As does the *CCC*, I suggest that much of what God is doing in this world can be described with the biblical image of the reign of God—a reign of justice, love, and peace. As seen in the life, preaching, teaching, dying, and rising of Jesus Christ, what God is up to is fashioning a new heaven and a new earth (see Revelation 21). But God does not work alone. We are intimately involved in what God is doing. The reign of God is and will be God's doing, but it is to happen in and through all of us, particularly those of us who are followers of Jesus Christ. God is tending the garden, but not without Mr. Piazza.

This chapter should be seen as the other side of the coin of chapter 1. In that chapter, we saw that the Christian moral life is, first and foremost, not about us, but about God. It is about the gift of God's love and how we attempt to respond to it. That remains true. But in the present chapter, the emphasis is in the other direction: Christian moral living is very much about what we do. It involves our active participation in God's work of fashioning a reign of justice, love, and peace. If the biblical image can be trusted, our active participation in God's work is so important that the garden will not blossom without it.

Still by way of introduction, another difference between this chapter and the previous one is one of emphasis. The previous chapter speaks predominately about responding to the gift of God's love. The current chapter emphasizes, more specifically, that the shape this response takes in the life of Christians is that of living in Christ. As the *CCC* reminds us, Christ is not present among us the way he was two thousand years ago. Through the power of the Spirit, he is present now through his Body, the Church. He is present now through you and me. The work of fashioning God's reign, seen in the life of Jesus Christ, is now entrusted to us, his followers.

But we are getting ahead of ourselves. In the pages that follow, we examine what Christian convictions about the reign of God have been and what active participation in that work entails. And then we take note of something I call "thisworldliness."

Christian Convictions About the Reign of God

Christian convictions about the reign of God are built upon the faith of Israel. So let us examine a Scripture passage that captures a good deal of the roots of Israel's belief about that reign: Exodus 3:7–10. In the story, the Israelites, enslaved in Egypt, have called out in prayer to God, pleading for God to do something on their behalf. In the following passage, God speaks to Moses and, through him, to the people of Israel.

> I have observed the misery of my people who are in Egypt; I have heard their cry on account of their taskmasters. Indeed, I know their sufferings, and I have come down to deliver them from the Egyptians, and to bring them up out of that land to a good and broad land, a land flowing with milk and honey. . . . The cry of the Israelites has now come to me; I have also seen how the Egyptians oppress them. So come, I will send you [Moses] to Pharaoh to bring my people, the Israelites, out of Egypt.

Jewish faith about the reign of God begins here. It begins with the belief that God not only hears us and cares about us, but—even more daring—God is willing to get involved, to "come down" to be with us and to act on our behalf. The story displays Israel's belief that God is deeply concerned about oppression and injustice. The implication of this for Israel became this: just as God has "come down" to do something about our situation of slavery and oppression, so, too, we must have a special concern and commitment to act on behalf of the poor or oppressed.

Note also that the story expresses Israel's faith about how God would act—not directly, but in and through Moses, in and through Israel. So God tells Moses to go to Pharaoh and to lead the people out of slavery. In the story, Moses protests: "Who am I that I should go to Pharaoh, and bring the Israelites out of

Egypt?" (Exodus 3:11). God responds not by giving Moses anything close to an action plan or a road map. Instead, God simply offers a promise: "I will be with you" (3:12).

What the Christian community believes about "the kingdom of God" or "the reign of God" is similar, but it centers on what we believe God was up to in the life and work, dying and rising of Jesus Christ. As does the *CCC* (see #714), let us look briefly at the following important passage from the Gospel of Luke:

> *The Spirit of the Lord is upon me,*
>> *because he has anointed me*
>>> *to bring good news to the poor.*
> *He has sent me to proclaim release to the captives*
>> *and recovery of sight to the blind,*
>>> *to let the oppressed go free,*
> *to proclaim the year of the Lord's favor.*

(4:18–19)

The words of Jesus here, a quotation from Isaiah 61:1–2, are a bold proclamation of Christian faith about Jesus Christ. The Spirit of God was upon Jesus in a unique and dramatic way. He was God's Son among us, and his mission was to bring good news to the poor, the afflicted, and the oppressed. Connecting this with the passage from Exodus, Christians believe that in and through the person and the work of Jesus Christ, God has "come down" to be with us. Not only has God been attentive to our needs, attentive to our brokenness and sinfulness, but, in Jesus, God has embraced them.

To be sure, Christians affirm that God's loving and saving presence was made manifest in the life of Israel, but we also believe that in sending his own Son to be among us, God has done something new. The reign of God has been established—not finished, but established—in a definitively new way. This belief is captured well by the evangelist Mark. In his Gospel, the very first words of Jesus are these: "The time is fulfilled, and the kingdom of God has come near; repent, and believe in the good news" (1:15).

By the phrase "kingdom of God" or "reign of God" Christians mean that what God was up to in Jesus Christ was establishing the definitive victory of grace over sinfulness, the victory of justice over oppression and, most dramatically, the victory of life over death. Note, Christian faith holds that this victory, this reign, has simply begun; it is hardly finished. We need only to look at the morning newspaper to be reminded that sin, oppression, and death are still with us. Nevertheless, Christians are those who hope for—indeed, await—the completion of Christ's victory, Christ's reign.

To put this a little differently, Christian faith provides believers with a view of history—indeed, a very hopeful one. God has been up to something for a long time. Glimpsed in the life of Israel and dramatized in the person and work of Jesus Christ—especially in and through his victory over death—God has been and remains up to the transformation of the human race and the fashioning of a new heaven and a new earth. That is quite an amazing claim. The first question for us is simply "Do we believe it? Do we think it is really possible, indeed, that it is really happening?" And the next question is "What is our role in this amazing work of God?" Let us proceed to respond to that question.

Christian Moral Life as Active Participation in Christ's Work of Building the Reign of God

There is obviously nothing subtle about the long title of this section. If the question is What is our role in the reign of God? the answer is We are called to active participation in what God is doing. In the paragraphs that follow, I suggest we reflect a bit on the meaning of the words *active* and *participation*. I propose that what participation requires of us is humility, and what being active requires of us is a sense of urgency.

To see oneself as a participant in Christ's work of building the reign of God, no doubt, requires a number of things. I suggest that among the most important requirements is a sense of genuine humility. I do not mean the caricature of humility that may come to mind—that false sense of humility that suggests "I'm really not worth all that much" or "I really don't have much to contribute." That is a far cry from what genuine humility is all about. Genuine humility is the virtue that enables us to see ourselves as we truly are; it is a virtue that enables us to be in touch with reality. In the light of Christian faith, persons of humility know that they are nothing less than children of God, created in the image and likeness of God (see Genesis 1:27; CCC, #356). Humble Christians believe this deeply. They know that because of their origin (in God) and because of their destiny (in God), they are creatures of enormous value, of inestimable worth. But, to recall something emphasized in chapter 1, they also know that this is all grace, all gift, and not the result of their own accomplishments, however valuable they may be. For Christian believers, this is where genuine humility begins.

But it does not stop there. To be humble and to be followers of Christ is to believe that God is up to something amazing: fashioning a reign of love and justice and peace. The humility of such persons would enable them never to forget that from the beginning to the end, it is God's work, God's reign. What we are called to do is to participate in what God is doing through the ways in which we live our lives, through the ways in which we work for love and justice and peace. But all the while, we do well to keep in mind the reality of this wonderful situation: it is God's doing, not ours. We must take part, and yes, our participation is essential. But fashioning a new heaven and a new earth is obviously a work "bigger" than any (or all) of us. It is "bigger" than what any (or all) of us can do.

Why is this important? It is important because this kind of humility—genuine Christian humility—can free us from the self-perfectionism that afflicts too many of us, the self-perfectionism that ultimately leads to depression, if not despair, because, in the end, we all fall short of being the perfect persons we somehow think we are supposed to be. Further, genuine Christian humility might help us all live with unfinished business. In our daily lives, how many of us struggle with hectic schedules, often frustrated at the end of the day by the fact that we didn't quite get it all done? And, more significant, how many of us struggle with the unfinished business of our world: with broken and seemingly "unfixable" relationships; with overwhelming social problems like poverty, hunger, and injustice; and with centuries-old hostilities and violence? Christian faith in the reign of God calls us to believe that however long it may take, however stubborn the forces of sin and suffering might be, God's reign, God's victory, is at hand; it is under way. To believe that involves risk, a risk that seems to border on foolishness. But, as the *CCC* suggests, such belief unleashes hope, hope in what God can do and in what God is already doing (see #1817–1821). That kind of hope must be based on humility, the ability to recognize the reality of our own worth as we contribute to what God is doing in this world.

If humility is essential to our ability to participate well in the building of God's reign, a sense of urgency is equally important for our active engagement in this faith-filled work. Perhaps a story may help here.

I remember my first theology lesson; my father was the teacher. It came many years ago when we were watching a Cleveland Indians baseball game on television. I must have been about seven or eight years old. Minnie Minoso stepped into the batter's box, and as he did, I saw that he made the sign of the cross. I had never noticed this before, so I said to my dad, "Did you see that, Dad? Minnie made the sign of the cross! Is that going to help him?" Without having to give it much thought, my theologian father responded, "Is that going to help him? Sure it is. It'll help him—as long as he came to batting practice, as long as he can hit!"

During his better moments (like this one), my father was a wise man—and he was very much a man of faith. What I learned in that first theology lesson is that God helps us, but that God needs us to help ourselves. We need to come to batting practice. We need to take the steps that we can take to get the job done.

God will be with us, God will help us, but God is not likely to do it for us. I suppose this is why I am so sympathetic with Mr. Piazza in the story that opened this chapter. The gardener does well to remember that both he and the garden exist in the first place because of the creative activity of God. The gardener does well to keep in mind that he is not the author of life. Even so, the gardener also knows that there is much work to be done in the garden, and even as he prays for good weather and good growth, he knows he must get to the tasks at hand—now.

So what does active participation in God's reign require? It requires a sense of urgency. It requires the ability to see the opportunities that are at hand—at our hands—to "step up to the plate," to do something today that may inch forward God's reign of justice, love, and peace. This is precisely what Moses was told when God sent him to Pharaoh to lead the people out of slavery in Egypt. Moses was being asked to believe that God would make it happen, and, at the same time, that it was not going to happen without his own leadership and decisive action. In other words, the reign of God is God's reign, and victory over sin and death will be won by the power of God—and, we are still called to action. Mrs. Farinacci had it right: God and Mr. Piazza had a beautiful garden. But Mr. Piazza also had it right: the garden becomes quite a mess when the gardener falls down on the job.

As we saw at the beginning of the chapter, Christian life is life in the Spirit. It is the ability to let God live in us and through us, the ability to believe that the reign of God will come about because of the power of the Spirit of God. But Christian life also entails being a witness.

In the Greek language, the language of the New Testament, the word witness and the word martyr are taken to be equivalent. To be a witness for Christ means acting in sometimes dramatic, costly ways. For some it has meant giving one's life for the sake of justice, love, and peace. Such witnesses dramatize the urgency that is involved in our active participation in the reign of God.

Christian Moral Life and "Thisworldliness"

The claim in this last section of the chapter is that our active participation in fashioning the reign of God has a certain "thisworldliness" about it. To understand what this means, let us look briefly at—of all people—Karl Marx.

Karl Marx (1818–1883) was a German philosopher whose ideas have been described as materialistic (denying the spiritual dimension of persons), deterministic (reducing human freedom to a minimum), and atheistic (denying the existence, or at least the relevance, of God). Deeply concerned about the plight of workers in Europe in his day—workers (including children) who spent long days laboring in unsafe factories for meager wages that did not come close to supporting their families, much less respect human dignity—Marx called for radical social change. So far, so good. But built into his philosophical and political ideas was a thoroughgoing criticism of religion, particularly Christianity, as "the opium of the people." Christian beliefs about heaven, he charged, distract people from seeing what is really going on in their world and keep them from doing anything about oppression and injustice. Like a drug, belief in "another world" dulls the senses of Christians and makes them willing to put up with social injustice in this world because, after all, it is the next world that is really important. Marx's criticism of Christianity is something I like to call "otherworldliness"; Christianity, he charged, spends too much effort focusing on "the next world" and not enough on this world.

It may be a matter of debate whether Marx's criticism had any real impact on Christianity. But what does not seem debatable historically is that not long after Marx, the Christian churches—including the Roman Catholic Church—began to pay much more attention to social ills like poverty, oppression, and injustice. In 1891, Pope Leo XIII issued an important encyclical, *Rerum Novarum (On the Condition of Workers)*, on the plight of workers and on the need for social reform. That letter began what is considered to be Catholicism's modern social justice teaching. Chapter 7 of this book explores that tradition. The point to emphasize here is simply this: Catholic social teaching has a definite "thisworldliness" about it. In the last hundred years, virtually every pope, from Leo XIII to John Paul II, has paid great attention to the social concerns of the day and has called for Christian people—individually, but especially corporately—to devote their energies to overcoming poverty, hunger, homelessness, discrimination, oppression, and violence. Catholicism seems to have heard the biblical teaching about the reign of God in a fresh way during this last century, in a way that seems marked by "thisworldliness." Just as Christ believed that the Spirit of God was upon him, calling him to deliver a message of hope to the poor, to bring freedom to those in captivity, to liberate those who were oppressed, so, too, in this century, Catholic teaching has emphasized that the same Spirit of God is upon us, that the mission of Christ is now ours. As the popes and bishops have been reminding us, we, too, must be about the business of contributing to Christ's work of love, justice, and peace in this world, for that is what God's reign is about.

Two further comments about "thisworldliness" are important. First, this way of viewing the Christian life—as active participation in the work of God's reign—calls attention to the continuity between this world and "the new heaven and the new earth" that God is fashioning. To be sure, there is discontinuity between this world and "the next world." This world is not heaven (in case we hadn't noticed) and, in fact, it will not one day simply become heaven as a result of our collective good work. For the reign of God to be brought to completion, God will have to act in a new and decisive manner. Nevertheless, the biblical image of the reign of God suggests that there is continuity between this world and the "new heaven and new earth" that will come to be. The reign of God is "at hand," it is already in our midst, the biblical authors insisted. In other words, this is not a "throw away" world. The reign of God will not replace our efforts and small victories of justice, love, and peace here and now;

rather, it will bring them to completion. What we do in this world matters; it is part of the much larger work of God.

Second, it is important to acknowledge several things that "thisworldliness" does not mean. It does not mean that our only obligations as Christians are those that relate directly to matters of social justice. The many, many pages in the *CCC* that discuss our obligations in regard to the Church itself or in regard to worship display the fact that Christianity is not simply about social concerns. In addition, to emphasize the "thisworldly" aspects of the reign of God and of Christian living does not at all suggest that in our daily lives we must become social activists. Many of us can identify important moral obligations arising from our relationships as parents, sons and daughters, brothers and sisters, friends, workers, etc. Some of us are healthy; some of us are ill and homebound. Some of us have positions of enormous influence in public life; many of us do not. So the ways in which we actively participate in God's work of fashioning a reign of justice, love, and peace are likely to vary greatly from person to person.

We must all care about our neighbor and, in the ways that are open to us, we must do what we can to contribute to God's work. We must tend the garden we are in.

Finally, to emphasize the "thisworldliness" of the reign of God and our active participation in it does not mean that there is no place for prayer. But perhaps, as it does in the season of Advent, our prayer might take two forms. We might do well to pray "Come, Lord Jesus" every day, praying for God to bring to completion that which was begun definitively in Jesus of Nazareth. And we might also pray that our eyes may be open, that we might recognize and respond to the opportunities that are "at hand" to help fashion the reign of God.

For Reflection

1. What are your reflections on the opening story of the chapter? Is God involved in what Mr. Piazza is doing in the garden? How? Is God active in this world? If so, how? How would you describe the relationship between what we do in this world and what God does in this world?

2. What comes to your mind when you hear the phrase "the reign of God"? Can you point to any events that seem to you to be signs that the reign of God is under way?

3. The chapter proposes that humility and a sense of urgency are essential qualities for those who would participate actively in the reign of God. What are some other qualities that seem necessary? Explain. Can you name some people in whom you see these qualities?

4. What do you think about the chapter's discussion of "this-worldliness"? Should not "otherworldliness" play a part in the life and spirituality of Christian persons? What dangers might there be with each of those ideas?

For Further Reading

Gula, Richard M., SS. "Jesus and Discipleship." Chap. 13 (pp. 195–198) in *Reason Informed by Faith: Foundations of Catholic Morality*. Mahwah, NJ: Paulist Press, 1989.

Hellwig, Monica. *Jesus: The Compassion of God*. Collegeville, MN: The Liturgical Press, 1983.

McBrien, Richard P. "Sacramentality" and "Mediation." Pages 9–12 in *Catholicism, Completely Revised and Updated*. San Francisco: HarperSanFrancisco, 1994.

Second Vatican Council. *Gaudium et Spes (Pastoral Constitution on the Church in the Modern World)*, 1965.

CHAPTER 3

Christian Morality and the Process of Conscience

"POP"

I
t's a time of uncertainty and hesitation, but also a time of decision. It's about Pop, as the world knows him. After his wife died four years ago, Pop, age eighty-three, went to live with the Andersons—Pop's daughter Lisa; her husband Joe; their seventeen-year-old daughter, Melissa; and their eleven-year-old son, Jason. Pop's been well: healthy, alert, independent, and even spunky in his sense of humor. Three weeks ago, however, he fell and broke his hip. Though Pop's surgery went well, his recovery is not following suit; he has had kidney failure, a collapsed lung, and signs of depression that are out of character and very hard for his family to face.

The hospital staff recommends a nursing home, but Pop never liked such places. The Andersons are wrestling with the idea of taking care of Pop at home. Maybe they could make the necessary adjustments in their lives. Should they? Doesn't love mean sacrifice? Or are their hearts getting in the way of logic? Could they really provide the best care for Pop? All this is hard on Melissa, Pop's favorite. Her parents have brought her into the decision-making process. She's glad of that, but like them, she's confused.

From the *Catechism:* Paragraphs 1778, 1783, 1785

Chapter 1 says that Christian morality is all about our effort to respond to the gift of God's love. We must try to love as God loves us. Chapter 2 suggests that the Christian moral life is also a life of active participation in the reign of God. We must respond to the opportunities that are at hand for us to help inch forward God's reign of justice, love, and peace.

This present chapter takes up one simple but important question: how? How can we know what "responding to God's love" would look like in specific situations? What is the genuinely loving thing to do, for example, in the story about Pop? How do we figure out the way to contribute to the reign of God in situations that seem to ooze with ambiguity? In other words, even if we are deeply appreciative of the gift of God's love and are driven by a desire to respond to that love in our daily lives, "how" may not always be obvious. Even if we believe deeply that God is fashioning a reign of justice, love, and peace, and that we must contribute to that reign, it may be far from clear just how we might do so in our daily lives as parents, spouses, attorneys, nurses, friends, citizens, and the like. Life is complicated.

Enter Catholic tradition's emphasis on conscience. Catholicism suggests that in and through the processes of conscience, all human persons try to figure out how to be good persons and how to do the right things. In and through conscience, we who are followers of Christ attempt to discern how we might respond to God's love and take part in God's reign in our daily lives. To be sure, to speak of conscience is not to speak of simple answers. There is no simple recipe for making good moral choices as Christians. But there is a way, a way that calls us to discern what we should do and who we might be when we are faced with difficult moral choices. That way, Catholic moral tradition suggests, is the way of conscience.

The *CCC*'s treatment of conscience, though not long, is important. The *CCC* acknowledges that we must follow our judgments of conscience and that we are responsible to inform our consciences as fully and authentically as possible. For, as we shall see, conscience has both a personal and a communal dimension.

Drawing on the *CCC* and also on the insights of a number of contemporary Catholic theologians who have written about three interrelated aspects of conscience (see the suggestions for further reading at the end of the chapter), let us reflect on conscience as a capacity, a process, and a judgment.

Conscience as Capacity for Goodness and Rightness

The word *conscience* means more than one thing. Over the centuries, Catholic philosophers and theologians have emphasized that one of the most important things the word *conscience* refers to is not something we do, but more deeply, something we are. We are creatures who have a capacity for goodness and rightness. We are capable of being good and of doing what is right. Connecting to what we have said about how we are created, we are fashioned in the image of God, we participate in the light of the Spirit of God. Through the use of our reason we are able to discover the proper order of the universe, and through the use of our free will we are free to make choices to live in accord with that order (see #1705).

These ideas reflect what might be called "Catholic optimism." They contrast with certain pessimistic philosophies of the early Church, views that suggested human beings were so riddled with darkness and evil that they were largely incapable of goodness. Catholicism's theology of creation suggests that despite sin, we remain created in the image and likeness of God. In contrast with the ideas of some of the reformers in the sixteenth century—most notably John Calvin and to a lesser extent, Martin Luther—Catholicism has insisted that human nature is fundamentally good. We are capable of goodness and rightness. And in contrast with certain contemporary philosophers and social scientists' belief that we are determined by our genetic endowments, family backgrounds, and our surrounding societies and cultures, Catholic tradition emphasizes that despite these powerful factors, we remain significantly free so that we can direct our lives to what is truly good (see #1704).

These are bold and confident Catholic convictions. They are an essential part of what our tradition means by saying that the most fundamental aspect of conscience is our capacity for being good and doing what is right. This drive for goodness and rightness is essential to what it means to be fully human. In fact, in those rare instances when it seems that this drive is lacking, when others seem to have no regard at all for goodness and rightness (or for the way their lives are affecting others), we often say that there is something "inhuman" about these persons. One clinical word for this type of person is *sociopath*; such people are dangerous to themselves and to others. The point seems simple, but it is of fundamental importance. We are capable of goodness and rightness. If one does not believe this, conversation about what conscience entails need not go further.

Two other points need to be made concerning "conscience as capacity." The first is that this capacity is developmental in nature. Our capacity for goodness and rightness is not given to us as a complete package when we are born. Rather, as a kind of moral muscle, our conscience awaits exercise and development. We are capable of developing ourselves as good persons, but that development is a lifelong project—arguably the most important one we ever undertake.

Obviously, then, we might expect that the capacity for goodness and rightness in the eighteen-year-old is more fully developed than in the eight-year-old. And, hopefully, the conscience of the sixty-eight-year-old—tested by the experience of moral success and moral failure—is marked by a higher degree of maturity and wisdom than that of the eight-year-old or even the eighteen-year-old.

All this should make it clear that the "conscience as capacity" of each of us is unique. We each have our own moral histories and experiences that have contributed to who we are—for good or for ill—and that influence how we face the moral questions in front of us at any given time. We each have our own moral character: our own configuration of convictions, attitudes, virtues, and vices that we draw on as we make our way through today's dilemmas. And we each find ourselves in a network of family relations, friendships, educational and work environments, and social, political, cultural, and religious communities that have made important contributions—again, for good or for ill—to the way we size up the moral situations in which we find ourselves. This is not to say that these factors determine who we are and what we will do. But it does dramatize that although "conscience as capacity" has a personal and unique dimension to it, it has a social and communal dimension as well.

A final point to make concerning "conscience as capacity" is a specifically spiritual one. In faith we are invited to believe that we not only have something to draw on in our moral struggles (our own moral muscle), but we have someone to draw on as well: the divine Spirit of God.

As emphasized in chapter 1, the Christian life is "life in the Spirit." All human persons, we believe, have been created in the image of God and have God's Spirit living within them. In Catholic tradition, this is the source of human dignity, the "place" where reverence for life begins. Hopefully, Christian people have made this conviction about God's Spirit front and center in their lives. We are invited to believe that the Spirit of God, the Spirit of Jesus Christ, abides in us in a way that both charges and enables us to be good and to do what is right. As it should be, this is a powerful source of support and hope for many Christian people. This does not mean that as they try to figure out what to do in regard to Pop, the Andersons don't need to get in touch with their best and deepest moral virtues and insights. Indeed, they do. But it means that they have a source of courage and wisdom that is larger than their own. When God sent Moses to Pharaoh to lead the people out of Egypt, he assured him, "I will be with you." This abiding presence of God's Spirit in our lives does not make the Christian moral life easy, but it makes it possible.

Conscience as Process: The Homework of Moral Decision Making

The first aspect of conscience, "conscience as capacity," is what we bring with us into every moral situation. It is the accumulation of experience and wisdom that serves as the backdrop for all of our moral decisions. Once we come upon a situation that calls for a moral judgment about what is the right thing to do—such as the Andersons' situation—the second aspect of conscience moves to center stage: conscience as process. Put very simply, this second aspect of conscience is what we do to prepare to make a good moral judgment. (As we will see, the judgment itself about what we must do is the third aspect of conscience.) This second aspect of conscience might be called "active conscience" for, indeed, here we must get busy; we must do our "homework" so that in the end the judgment we make will be the fruit of our best moral reflection.

Just what are some of the things we might do in the "process of conscience"? (Before reading any further, perhaps it would be helpful to answer this question for yourself. When you have been faced with an important moral judgment and decision, what are some of the things you have done that have helped you?) The *CCC* suggests that in concrete situations, as we try to determine God's will for us, we do well to seek the help of trusted others, of competent people, for, indeed, the voice of the Spirit of God is often at work in and through those around us (see #1787, 1788).

This is very wise. We must try to discern what God wants us to do by interpreting the data of experience, the signs of the times, the advice of competent people, and the help of the Holy Spirit. In an effort to make these suggestions even more specific, here is my own proposal for things that might be good to do in virtually all situations:

1. Identify the moral judgment to be made.

2. Gather relevant information.

3. Seek counsel.

4. Evaluate alternatives.

5. Reflect and pray.

A brief reflection on each of these interrelated and often overlapping tasks seems in order.

Identify the moral choice to be made. Perhaps it seems too obvious to be necessary, but the truth is that some moral judgments are not made well because a clear focus concerning the moral judgment is lacking from the outset. Put differently, all moral judgments involve a question, and the way the question is framed may set the stage for making a judgment very well or very poorly. For example, if the Andersons are wrestling with the question "How can we best love Pop in this situation?" their struggle may display the constancy of their love for Pop, but the question itself may not really be helpful. It may be so general that they will have a hard time answering it, or it may prejudice them in the direction of rearranging their lives so that they can take care of Pop at home, presuming that doing so would be the most loving thing to do. Maybe.

A different question is "How can we see to it that Pop gets the best care possible at this time in his life?" The focus of this question seems more on Pop and less on the Andersons. It seems to be a more open question than the previous one, one that moves them to seek out what really is in Pop's best interest in a more even-handed way. The point is that the way we identify the moral choice to be made is important. It gets the process of moral investigation going—hopefully, in a clear and unbiased way.

Gather relevant information. A large part of good moral decision making involves gathering good and relevant information. Depending on the nature of the moral situation, the types of information needed may vary greatly. The Andersons will need information from a variety of medical professionals. They need to understand the precise kind of care Pop is likely to need, what kind of expertise is required to provide it, how long it will have to be provided, and so on. No doubt they will also need information from nursing homes and insurance agencies about the short-term and long-term costs that will be involved. And, of course, there is Pop himself. Centrally important information includes his own wishes, including his present capacity for communicating with them. So there are a lot of things to find out in a relatively short period of time. In other situations, other types of information will be needed, but in all cases, good decisions must be based on good information.

Seek counsel. As we have seen, the *CCC* suggests that as we try to discern the right thing to do, as we seek to discern God's will for us, we do well to seek and interpret "the advice of competent people" (#1788). Obviously this overlaps with the previous point; we must gather our information from competent people. But I propose three other ways in which seeking counsel is important.

First, it is often wise to consult with others who have faced similar moral judgments. Even with all the things that are unique about the Andersons and their situation, they are not the first family to struggle over how to provide quality care for an elderly loved one. There may be a wealth of experience and wisdom that the Andersons would do well to take advantage of.

Second, when we face a difficult moral decision we are also wise to consult with someone who knows us well. It often makes great sense to talk with someone who knows a bit about our moral strengths and weaknesses, someone who might help us get in touch with our strongest virtues and our deepest wisdom, someone who might help us avoid the "shadow side" of our personality and character. In difficult moral situations, such trusted others can be invaluable sources of help. Such persons are nothing less than gifts of God.

And a third aspect of "seeking counsel" in the Catholic tradition that deserves a special word concerns the place of official Catholic teachings. As we will see in chapters 5, 6, and 7—the chapters on Catholic medical, sexual, and social teachings—the Catholic Church has developed a body of teachings on specific moral issues that can be a special source of wisdom to Catholics (and others) as they try to discern the right thing to do in a given situation. Some of those teachings are general (our call to respect life, for example); others are specific (direct or active euthanasia is always objectively wrong, for example). As the *CCC* teaches, it is expected that as Catholics, we allow ourselves to be guided by the teachings of the Church on moral questions (see #1785) as we try to discern the right thing to do. The Church does not make moral judgments and decisions for us. If that were the case, then conscience would simply be a matter of finding out what the moral law or rule is and then being obedient to it. But that is not what conscience is about, nor is it what Catholic teaching is for. Rather, its purpose is to assist us, to guide us as we try to identify our own moral obligations here and now.

Evaluate alternatives. As the process of conscience and moral decision making proceeds, it often happens—especially if we have acquired good information and received wise counsel—that a number of alternatives emerge. This isn't always the case, however; sometimes the alternatives have an either-or quality about them. For example, after a long process of discernment, a woman in an abusive marital relationship may be faced, in the end, with the decision of whether or not to seek a separation from her spouse. Sometimes moral judgments are that stark—but not always. Often it is the case, after information has been obtained and counsel has been sought, that what appeared to be an either/or situation turns out to be one with a much wider spectrum of alternatives. The Andersons, for example, might find out that two of the options they had not considered involve Pop going to a nursing home for a few weeks for rehabilitation and then coming to their home afterwards, or Pop coming to their home right away, but with nursing assistance at home, some of which might be covered by Pop's insurance plan. As the alternatives expand, there is often an opportunity to turn what appeared to be an either/or, win/lose situation into one marked by a greater degree of win/win. People of experienced moral wisdom are often able to recognize alternatives that were not clear at the start. They are people with good imaginations.

Reflect and pray. The section on conscience in the *CCC* begins with this quote from one of the Second Vatican Council documents:

> Deep within his conscience man discovers a law
> which he has not laid upon himself but which he

must obey. Its voice, ever calling him to love and to do what is good and to avoid evil, sounds in his heart at the right moment. . . . For man has in his heart a law inscribed by God. . . . His conscience is man's most secret core and his sanctuary. There he is alone with God whose voice echoes in his depths.

(Gaudium et Spes, #16)

What a wonderful image! Our conscience is our secret core and sanctuary. It is that "holy place" within us where the voice and Spirit of God are to be found. And it is the "place" within us where our most important and best moral judgments and decisions are made. If, as we have said, the Christian moral life is life in the Spirit, then it should be obvious that when we are faced with a difficult moral decision, we do ourselves a favor to get in touch with the abiding presence of the Spirit of God within us. We should pray. To be clear, the Spirit of God does not make decisions for us. But if our hearts are open, the Spirit of God is capable of enlightening and empowering us. The Spirit can enlighten us so that we might see ourselves with clarity and wisdom. And, just as important, the Spirit can empower us so that we might act courageously on what we have come to recognize as our moral obligation. Those who strive for moral wisdom do well to visit the sanctuary often.

Conscience as Judgment: Taking Responsibility

The third aspect of conscience is what emerges from the process of conscience we have just described, namely, the concrete moral judgment about what one must do in a given situation. Indeed, it is a centuries-old Catholic conviction that we must act in accord with our conscience, with what we have judged to be our concrete moral obligation. Three reflections on this Catholic conviction are important.

First, this teaching about conscience is really a call for a high degree of maturity and responsibility. The moral life, the *CCC* suggests, entails far more than paying attention to the rules and regulation of the Church or society and being obedient to them in some mechanical manner. Moral maturity means taking responsibility for one's actions, for one's life. Our actions are expressions of who we are; they say something about the quality of our character. And at the same time, they are formative of the persons we are becoming. That is, they have a kind of "boomerang effect" in that they come back to us, influencing our character, for good or ill. This is what the *CCC* means by saying that freedom of conscience is important so that personally we can make moral decisions. Yes, it is good news: we must enjoy freedom of conscience so that we can live our own lives. And yes, it is challenging good news: freedom of conscience is a clarion call for responsibility and moral maturity.

Second, Catholic teaching about conscience—specifically about freedom of conscience—presumes that responsible and mature persons are attentive to both the personal and the communal aspects of the moral life. So the *CCC* stresses that as persons we must enjoy freedom of conscience so that our actions can truly be our own. At the same time, the *CCC* stresses that persons with a responsible and mature conscience will pay careful attention to the guidance and wisdom of the communities of which they are a part. We must be free to act in accord with our conscience, and at the same time, we must see to it that our conscience has been enlightened by the wisdom of others. Freedom of conscience is an invitation to be ourselves, while the duty to form our conscience is an invitation to recognize that we are not isolated from others. We are parts of communities, and we are responsible for the ways our actions either help or hinder what is good for others. To be a person is to be connected with others. There are few things that are more central to Catholic thinking than that conviction.

Third, if it is true that our conscience is sacred, that respect for freedom of conscience is an important part of respect for human dignity, it is also true that conscience is frail. We can make mistakes; we can miss the mark. In other words, to say that we must act in accord with our judgments of conscience is not to say that our judgments will always be right. Our conscience may be misinformed; we may have "moral blind spots" that can result in our actions causing significant harm to ourselves and others. Some of these blind spots may be peculiar to ourselves, such as my own particular stubbornness or closed-mindedness on an issue that keeps me from seeing things as they really are. Some blind spots may be shared with others; they may be part of one's culture. One might think of racism or sexism here. Such prejudicial thought patterns and attitudes can prevent us from seeing our relationships with others as they truly are. They can result in actions and structures of injustice and oppression that have devastating effects on others, even if they do not arise from hearts that are malicious and evil. Sometimes ignorance is all that is needed for bad things to happen.

The *CCC* discusses all of this in several paragraphs that have the subtitle "Erroneous Judgment" (see #1790–1794). Sometimes one's erroneous judgment may "be imputed to personal responsibility" (#1791); we may be culpable precisely because we expended little or no effort to form our conscience thoroughly. At other times, our errors of judgment do not indicate moral irresponsibility or sinfulness, because we did the best we could to form our conscience, even though we ended up doing something that was objectively wrong (see #1793). It is wise to refrain from trying to pinpoint the degree of moral culpability of others; such judgments are best left to one far wiser—and far more compassionate—than we are.

This concluding point about the frailty of conscience need not lead us to revise what we have said about the sanctity of conscience. But if it leaves us with a certain degree of humility in regard to our moral judgments and convictions, if it leaves us with the conclusion that our conscience should not only be respected, but monitored, it will be a point worth remembering.

For Reflection

1. What does the word *conscience* mean to you? What images come to mind when you hear the word?

2. What reflections, questions, or comments do you have about this chapter's discussion of "Catholic optimism"? Do you share it? Explain.

3. Think of someone you admire—especially someone you admire as a good moral person. Try to describe that person's capacity for goodness and rightness. What are some of the things that seem to have helped this person develop such a fine capacity for goodness and rightness?

4. Recall an important moral decision you have faced. What are some of the things you found yourself doing as you prepared to make a good moral judgment? What was helpful? What wasn't so helpful? How does your experience compare to what was proposed in the chapter's discussion of the second aspect of conscience: "conscience as process"?

5. The chapter suggests that we must be free to act in accord with our conscience. It also emphasizes that this requires a high degree of responsibility and maturity. Drawing on your own experience, is "freedom of conscience" important to you? Why or why not? What do the phrases "moral responsibility" and "moral maturity" mean to you?

For Further Reading

Connors, Russell B. Jr., and Patrick T. McCormick. *Character, Choices & Community: The Three Faces of Christian Ethics.* Mahwah, NJ: Paulist Press, 1998. (See especially chapter 7, "Conscience: Doing the Truth," and chapter 8, "Conscience Formation.")

Gula, Richard M., SS. *Reason Informed by Faith: Foundations of Catholic Morality.* Mahwah, NJ: Paulist Press, 1989. (See especially chapters 9, 10 and 11: "Conscience," "The Formation of Conscience," and "Conscience and Church Authority," respectively.)

O'Connell, Timothy E. *Principles for a Catholic Morality.* Rev. ed. San Francisco: HarperSanFrancisco, 1990. (See especially chapter 9, "Conscience.")

Overberg, Kenneth R., SJ. *Conscience in Conflict: How to Make Moral Choices.* Cincinnati: St. Anthony Messenger Press, 1991.

CHAPTER 4

Christian Morality and the Dynamics of Sin and Conversion

ANGELA

♦♦ "It's a miracle—that's the only word for it." That's how Angela described it to us some weeks ago. We all knew that Angela's bout with alcoholism had been an ordeal not only for her, but for her family and friends as well. We were relieved and thrilled for her when she was finally able to stick it out at the treatment center. We admired the way she stuck with her program in AA. But this conversation made it clear that we really hadn't appreciated the significance of this for Angela, how deeply this experience has changed her life.

"I was on a death march," Angela said, "literally, I was headed for death. I hated you for it at the time, of course, but I know now that the night you orchestrated that intervention and almost literally dragged me to the hospital was the most graced moment of my life. That darkest of moments was, at the same time, the beginning of the resurrection of my life. I also believe that I'm only one drink away from death. I pray that I never forget that."

When Angela finished talking, there was a silence that seemed to last a long time. Melissa finally spoke up, saying simply, "Angela, you're the greatest; we love you." The conversation moved on, but I suspect none of us have forgotten the power and grace of Angela's words that night.

From the *Catechism:* Paragraphs 1428, 1848, 1850, 1865

In the introduction to this book, I tell a story about a friend who liked to tease me about what I study and teach: Christian morality, "the dark side of the Good News." I suppose the contents of this chapter might be what he had in mind. It's partially true: to talk about sin and the wounded side of human existence is often not pleasant. So be on guard; this chapter might invite you to get in touch with some of those nooks and crannies of your life that you're glad not too many people know about. And talk about conversion—the idea that we need to be changed, that we sometimes need to "turn around"—may be equally uncomfortable. In spite of all this, I hope you read on.

It is only partially true that conversation about sin and conversion is difficult. In Christian faith, sin is an opportunity to talk about grace, and conversion is an invitation to proclaim a much more powerful and hopeful conviction: we can be made whole; the process is already under way. In light of the resurrection of Jesus Christ, the final words of the conversation are not sin and death, but grace and life. Ask Angela, the hero-saint in this chapter's opening story. To be clear, the point of her story is not that alcoholism is a sin. Fortunately, today we understand that alcoholism is a disease—indeed, a potentially life-threatening disease. But Angela would have us know that if alcoholism is not about human sinfulness for which one is guilty, it is about brokenness and woundedness, and surely it cries out for the processes of healing and conversion that this chapter discusses. As Angela would tell us, conversion is both hard work and a gift.

In this chapter we first discuss "original sin" and "actual sin," noting, as theologian Timothy O'Connell has put it, that in some ways "sin is a fact," and in other ways "sin is an act." Second, we look at conversion, and, as the New Testament does, I propose that it is good to think of conversion not as a command, but as a possibility. Third, we reflect briefly on the foundation of this hopeful perspective on sin and conversion, namely the resurrection of Jesus Christ.

Sin: "Original" and "Actual"

What are the first three things that come to your mind when you hear the word "sin"? [Take a minute to answer this question before you read further.] Based upon my experience in undergraduate classrooms and in a variety of settings for adult education, if you are like a lot of people, there is a good chance your answers might include things like cheating, stealing, lying, murder, adultery, and so on. Those are good answers. Indeed, sin has a great deal to do with specific actions we perform that are just plain wrong—not just mistakes, but wrong in the moral sense, out of keeping with what human beings ought to do, and surely out of keeping with what it means to be a follower of Christ. Sin is about what we do; "sin is an act."

But, following Tim O'Connell's lead, it is valuable to reflect on a dimension of human sinfulness that seems even more fundamental than the idea that "sin is an act"—namely, "sin is a fact." Sin is not simply about what we do. In an insidious and more pervasive way, sin is "bigger" than that. It is about the woundedness of the world. It is about the way that all things, especially we ourselves, are not quite right, whether it be in the small imperfections that frustrate all of us or in the hideousness of full-blown hatred and evil that sometimes cause us to tremble. "Sin is a fact," and it has been that way from the start. The Catholic tradition addresses this with the doctrine of "original" sin.

ORIGINAL SIN

In the first part of the *CCC*, the section that explains "The Profession of Faith," sin is described generally as an abuse of the freedom that God gives to created persons so that they are capable of loving him and loving one another (#387).

We are created in the image and likeness of God, and this is dramatized especially in our powers of intelligence and freedom. But we are capable of abusing those powers. And that is precisely what sin is about: using our intelligence in ways that distort the truth, and using our freedom to go our own way rather than God's. Sin of every sort entails rebellion against God.

What is particular about the notion of original sin is that this attempted rebellion of humankind against God has been going on from the beginning, and it is passed down from one generation to the next. The story of "the fall" of Adam and Eve from chapter 3 of Genesis is an attempt to explain, in figurative language, some important event that took place at the beginning of humankind's history, an original fault by "our first parents" that has influenced humankind ever since (see #390).

According to this great story, the harmony that marked the "original" experience of Adam and Eve was disrupted by their sin. The rebellion of the first human beings introduced into the world forces of evil that are not easily overcome. And, unfortunately, we all now inherit a world that is marked by this lack of harmony. It influences us from the very beginning of our lives; it "gets into our bones." We are still created in God's image, and we are still fundamentally good, but because of original sin, knowing what is true and freely doing what is right do not come easily.

It seems unfair, doesn't it? We inherit the "fallout" from the sinful, rebellious deeds of those who have gone before us. We get what we don't deserve. But there is another side to this. The *CCC* urges that we never forget the Good News of the gift of salvation offered to us all through Jesus Christ (see #398).

We need to keep in mind that God's offer of salvation is made to sinners. It is not something we have earned; rather it is purely and simply a gift. So we do well to keep in mind that if original sin is not something we deserve, neither is salvation!

ACTUAL SIN

Original sin is not the whole story. If we inherit a world in which "sin is a fact," we eventually learn how to make it our own. In and through the deeds we sometimes perform—deeds that are marked in a variety of ways by selfishness, dishonesty, and injustice—we make our own contribution to the sin of the world. "Sin is an act." So in addition to what we inherit, we do things large and small that sometimes display a lack of love and care for ourselves, for one another, and for God.

In a way that is both traditional and seems to correspond with common sense, the *CCC* describes both mortal sin and venial sin (see #1854). The difference lies in their severity and in their effect upon us.

Mortal sin is a violation of God's law that is so serious that it destroys the life of grace within us. It turns us away from God (see #1855). In order to commit a mortal sin the act itself must be seriously wrong, and it must be committed with full knowledge and full consent of the will (see #1857).

There are some important things to note here. Most important, mortal sin is not casual. We can theorize about how often we might commit mortal sin, but it is not something we do off-handedly and probably not something most of us do regularly. As the word "mortal" suggests, this kind of sin kills God's life in us—not because God stops loving us, but because we turn our back on God in what we do.

Note also how the *CCC* stresses that in order for someone to commit such a sin three things must be in place. First, the deed itself must be seriously wrong. This is what the text means by saying that the "object" must involve grave matter. Second, the person must have full knowledge of the seriously wrong nature of the act. Third, the person must perform the action with "complete consent," that is, with full freedom. In #1859 and #1860, the *CCC* points out that a person may do something seriously wrong (actions that Catholic teaching calls "objectively wrong"), but the person may do so with a lesser degree of knowledge of its wrongness or with a lesser degree of freedom. In those instances, there would be a lesser degree of sinfulness; the action would not be a mortal sin, but perhaps a venial sin. It could even be that a person's knowledge or freedom was diminished so thoroughly that even though the person did something "objectively" wrong, perhaps seriously harmful to that person's self or to others, there might not be any degree of personal sinfulness at all.

The upshot of this is that we are wise to avoid making judgments about the sinfulness of others. We may observe others doing something wrong, but we do not have access to the hearts of others; we do not have the ability to assess the knowledge and freedom of others as they do what they do. I say thank God for this. Thank God—our compassionate and forgiving God—that we are not in the business of making these kinds of judgments about others. It is hard enough to do so for ourselves!

Venial sin, the *CCC* explains (more briefly), wounds our relationship with God, but does not destroy it (see #1855). While mortal sin entails turning our back on God, venial sin is less dramatic. Venial sin does not destroy our relationship with God, but it weakens it. Just as in a marriage or a good friendship, there can be all sorts of actions that display selfishness, insensitivity, and taking the other for granted. Such things might not "bring the relationship down," but they certainly won't help it. In fact, such patterns of behavior can pave the way to a rupture in the relationship that turns out to be "mortal." To be sure, in some ways, venial sin seems part of daily life. We all know what it's like to be both on the giving and receiving end of insensitivity and selfishness. But if this is the case, then forgiveness also needs to be part of our daily lives. We ought not take venial sin lightly, but we ought not "beat ourselves up" over it either, nor should we do so to others. A sense of humor and the ability to forgive are in order.

There is one more thing to note about sin. The result of both original sin and of our own personal sins has brought about what can be called the sin of the world (see John 1:29). This refers to the way that human sinfulness "shows up" in the fabric of our communities, in our social structures, and in our customary patterns of relating to one another (see #408).

This isn't good news, but it is true. Sin is not only a personal affair; rather, it has an insidious social dimension as well. Injustice, prejudice, and sometimes centuries-old hostilities and violence are part of the landscape we call "this world." Questions like Who's to blame? Who's at fault? Who started all this? Who sinned? are usually not helpful. This kind of sinfulness is "bigger" than any of us. As the *CCC* notes (and as Pope John Paul II often does in his writing), the social dimension of sin is often displayed in the social structures of our communities and cultures. For example, racism and slavery were once "factored in" to the structures and laws of our nation. Apartheid was not simply a personal attitude, but the way of doing business in South Africa. Sexism and other types of "isms" are often part and parcel of the laws, norms, and customs in our communities. All of this is part of "the sin of the world." It's overwhelming, isn't it? Fortunately, this is far from the end of the story.

Conversion as Command and Possibility

Let us return to Angela. Her words to her friends in our opening story capture a good deal of what this section of the chapter tries to explain. Angela said that for her it was the "darkest of moments." She thought she was coming over to a friend's house for a birthday celebration for a coworker. It turned out to be something very different. When she arrived, family and friends were there waiting for her, and with them there was someone she did not know, someone, she would soon learn, from the hospital's rehabilitation center for alcohol and drug abuse.

The "intervention" was motivated by the concern and love of her family and friends, but in that moment, it was devastating. Angela thought she had been rather good at keeping her addiction behind the closed doors of her life. But she found out that night how sadly she had been kidding herself. Each of her friends—including two of her sisters—described in painful detail some of the occasions when it was all too evident that her drinking was out of control: the falls, the bruises, the car accident, the absences from work, and so on. These things hadn't been missed. But it was so painful to hear the litany of them all. Angela was beyond embarrassed; she was driven to the hospital that night feeling naked, empty, and alone.

But we know how the story turned out. Today Angela describes that "darkest of moments" as "the most graced moment" in her life. Beginning that night at her friend's house, Angela started to learn—grudgingly and gradually—that she, in fact, was not alone. With the help of others and with the grace of God, she would eventually become convinced that there was a path that could lead her out of the dark and cold tomb in which she had been living. She has traveled down that path. Eleven years—and who knows how many AA meetings—later she is a changed person. And she knows "it's a miracle."

What is conversion? Angela's story captures a great deal of it. The call to conversion—the call to change—is not only a command, it is a possibility.

As we noted in the discussion of the reign of God in chapter 2, the first words out of the mouth of Jesus in the Gospel of Mark are, "The time is fulfilled, and the kingdom of God has come near; repent, and believe in the good news" (Mark 1:15). That is both good news and bad news. The bad news is that we must own up to our sinfulness. The good news is that accepting our sinfulness is, at the very same time, the gift of the Holy Spirit who leads us to a new life. Pope John Paul II explains this twofold dynamic of sin and conversion extremely well.

> Conversion requires convincing of sin; it includes the interior judgment of conscience, and this, being a proof of the action of the Spirit of truth in man's inmost being, becomes at the same time the start of a new grant of grace and love: "Receive the Holy Spirit"
>
> (*Dominum et Vivificantem*, #31).

To say this simply, conversion is not only a command, but a possibility. Perhaps there is no story in the New Testament that better captures this insight about the command and possibility of conversion than the story of the woman caught in adultery, found in chapter 8 of John's Gospel. (It may be valuable at this point to pause for a moment and read that story from the Gospel.) Reading between the lines of the story, it is not hard to imagine the woman feeling that "it's all over." The experience of guilt and public shame must have been overwhelming. She found herself the object of scorn, a pawn in the confrontational dialogue between Jesus and the religious leaders.

In addition, she was on the short end of a serious sexist injustice: where was the man, her accomplice? She was alone, ashamed, and empty, perhaps saying to herself, "Please, go right ahead: throw the stones. My future is gone, my life is over, let's get this over with."

But instead she encountered Jesus, and she left with the possibility of a future. "You may go," Jesus said to her rather simply, "You may go." Of course, she had a long way to go to put her life back together, but she was told that from that darkest of moments she could move on, she could begin again. Yes, she must go; she must avoid this sin again. But the good news was that she *could* go. If there is a more hopeful word in the entire New Testament than the word "go" in this story, I am not sure what it is. "Go" is not only a command, but a possibility.

The story does not tell us anything further about this woman, about what happened to her later, so we are left to wonder. If she were to try to move on from this experience, how would she do it? Taking a cue from the story about Angela, it seems certain that she would not move on alone. She would do so with the help of other people, for most often we are the instruments of God's grace for one another.

Christ's transforming grace is operative and at work in our lives, enabling us to have hope in dark moments, to begin again. And the way that this happens, most often, is in and through one another. Angela cannot tell the story of her road back from alcoholism without telling of the people who first challenged her to move on and then showed her the way to do so. This demonstrates well one of the most fundamental convictions of Christian faith: God saved us from our sin in and through the life and work of Jesus Christ. Now, through the power of the Holy Spirit, that saving grace of Christ is mediated to us in and through one another.

It is important to end these reflections on conversion by calling attention to the social nature of conversion. Many of the examples used so far in this chapter have been about the dynamics of sin and conversion in the lives of individual persons. That is probably where we encounter sinfulness and the call to conversion most deeply. But it would be misleading to end the conversation there. The *CCC* points out something that is as important as inner conversion: For conversion to be complete it must involve a transformation of our human structures and institutions, for these, as we have seen, are also marked by human sinfulness (see #1888).

The reign of God, as we have seen, is not simply about the transformation of persons, but about the transformation of this world into God's reign of justice, love, and peace. The dynamics of sin and grace describe not only what can happen in human hearts, but what God intends for the world itself. God intends that human communities and cultures, riddled at times with injustice and violence, be transformed. The very structures and institutions of our society that bear the marks of human sinfulness call out for conversion.

Is this possible? Admittedly, the massiveness and extensiveness of social injustice and violence make it seem that the possibility of social conversion is remote, perhaps only a fantasy. But then we do well to notice what has happened in places like South Africa in recent decades. The social transformation there is far from complete, but, indeed, what has happened there has been dramatic. If we are "on the watch," we might notice that the process of social conversion is under way in other places and in other ways. If our eyes are open, we might notice the way that both personal and social conversions are close "at hand," both as command and as possibility.

Resurrection Faith and Christian Hope

Not unlike the discussion of the reign of God in chapter 2, this chapter argues that conversion from sin to grace, both personally and socially, is not only a command but a possibility. There is obviously something hopeful about this idea, but it seems important to ask, "Is it real or simply wishful thinking? What is the basis of our hope?"

Christian faith does not hesitate in its response to this question. The basis of Christian hope—the foundation of the hopeful Christian belief that we not only must but can be transformed from sin to grace and from death to new life—is nothing other than the resurrection of Jesus Christ. Paul's First Letter to the Corinthians reminds us: If Christ has not been raised, then our preaching is in vain and your faith is in vain (1 Corinthians 15:14; see also *CCC*, #651).

Christian faith begins with the belief that Christ has been raised from the dead, and so the preaching of the Good News that we can be transformed is not at all in vain.

There seems to be only one question left: Do we believe it? Do we really believe in the Resurrection? And if so, just what is it that we believe? I propose that there are three things that faith in the resurrection of Christ invites us to believe. They each have something to do with the image of the empty tomb.

The first thing that resurrection faith is obviously about is the resurrection of Jesus Christ from the dead. It is the central mystery of Christian faith (see #638).

Recall the Gospel story we hear proclaimed on Easter Sunday about the women coming to the tomb to anoint the body of the dead Jesus. What they encountered was an empty tomb and the angel asking them, "Why do you look for the living among the dead? He is not here, but has risen" (Luke 24:5). Resurrection faith begins with a conviction about what happened to Jesus; no tomb was deep enough or strong enough to hold in the Son of God. The Resurrection is a confirmation of the works and teachings of Christ and, indeed, a confirmation of his own divinity (see *CCC*, #651, 653).

But if resurrection faith stops there, it stops far too soon. A second—and even more amazing—aspect of the Easter story that we are invited to believe is not about Christ's resurrection, but our own. Paul's First Letter to the Corinthians puts it this way, "For as all die in Adam, so all will be made alive in Christ" (1 Corinthians 15:22).

Easter faith is not only about the empty tomb of Jesus; it is about our empty tombs as well. What a startling, bold claim! Dare we believe it? Those who live in Christ share the same destiny as Christ. Those who live a life of love await the final embrace of the God who is love. If you have ever wept at a grave and walked away with the conviction that your loved one was not there, that the cold, dark earth was not your loved one's final destiny, but instead believed that person has been transformed and is living now with God, then you've got it—you've got what this second stage of resurrection faith is all about. Death did not have the final word for Jesus, and it does not have the final say for us either. Our tombs can be empty.

But that is not all. Easter faith invites something else. Be advised, however, that this third aspect of resurrection faith is not for the weak of heart. It is deeply hopeful, to be sure, but deeply challenging as well. This is the aspect of resurrection faith that Angela was telling her friends about as she recalled that her darkest hour was, at the same time, the beginning of her resurrection.

What Angela seems to understand deeply is that the Resurrection is not simply about what happened to Jesus a long time ago, and it is not simply about what will happen to us at the end of our lives. Rather, it is about what we are willing to let happen to us today. The fullness of faith in the Resurrection is the ability to believe that the dark tombs we live in today—tombs of sin, fear, resentment, hostility, injustice—can be made empty. It is the ability to believe that through the Holy Spirit, the power of the risen Christ is at work in us now, and that through this power we can be raised up from all that "entombs" us, from all that prevents us from being who we are capable of being, personally and communally.

Jesus Christ, the risen one, is alive in us (see *CCC*, #655), and it is the life of this risen one, what we have called the life of grace, that enables us to live new lives here and now. As Angela would want to remind us, we are not talking about magic here. (In Dietrich Bonhoeffer's words, there is no "cheap grace.") Letting ourselves be transformed from "brokenness" to "wholeness" is not easy, does not happen overnight, and always requires our steadfast, determined cooperation. But such transformation is "at hand"; it is a possibility here and now. People of Easter faith are those who believe that such conversions have everything to do with the grace of the risen Christ that has been unleashed and is at work among us—today.

For Reflection

1. How did you answer the question, "What are the first three things that come to your mind when you hear the word *sin*?" (see page 46). Do you think you would answer this question differently now in light of this chapter? If so, how?

2. What does the opening story of Angela have to do with sinfulness? Surely the idea is not that alcoholism is a sin; we have come to see it as a kind of disease. How, then, is her story related to this chapter? At one point, Angela was referred to as a "hero-saint." Does this describe her? If so, how?

3. The chapter discusses the possibility of someone doing something seriously wrong without necessarily committing a mortal sin. Can you think of an example of this? What seems helpful about this distinction? What might be dangerous about it?

4. The chapter argues that conversion is not simply a command, but a possibility. Does this seem right? If so, tell a story that captures this insight.

5. What do you believe about the Resurrection? Do you think about it mostly as a future event? Can you give an example—from your own life or someone else's—about the difference belief in the Resurrection can make for one's life here and now?

For Further Reading

Connors, Russell B. Jr., and Patrick T. McCormick. *Character, Choices & Community: The Three Faces of Christian Ethics*. Mahwah, NJ: Paulist Press, 1998. (See especially chapter 11, "Sin and Morality," and chapter 12, "Christian Moral Conversion.")

Hanigan, James P. "Conversion and Christian Ethics." Pages 242–251 in *Introduction to Christian Ethics: A Reader*. Edited by Ronald P. Hamel and Kenneth R. Himes, OFM. Mahwah, NJ: Paulist Press, 1989.

O'Connell, Timothy E. *Principles for a Catholic Morality*. Rev. ed. San Francisco: HarperSanFrancisco, 1990. (See especially chapter 7, "The Theology of Sin.")

O'Keefe, Mark, OSB. *What Are They Saying About Social Sin?* Mahwah, NJ: Paulist Press, 1990.

Peck, M. Scott. *People of the Lie: The Hope for Healing Human Evil*. New York: Simon and Schuster, 1983.

CHAPTER 5

Christian Morality and Issues of Health and Life

Andrew

Andrew has AIDS. He is only eight years old. AIDS in children like Andrew causes one either to scream or to be silent—it is a cruel mismatch if ever there was one. His is a sad, familiar story: cardiac problems combined with hemophilia, transfusions in the first months of life, infections, fevers, and so on and on, leading to the diagnosis: HIV+. All that was several years ago. The course of his health has deteriorated since then. The drug Azidothymidine (AZT) was effective for a time, but now Andrew is losing ground: "wasting away" or "failing to thrive," as they say. The physicians have spoken of newer treatments that might be tried: experimental, to be sure, but with some signs of effectiveness, so, certainly, some hope. Of course, there would be risks, but then, things are not hopeful for Andrew long-term. What really is best for Andrew?

Aunt Mabel

Aunt Mabel, age seventy-four, suffered a severe stroke five weeks ago and has been in the intensive care unit since then—hooked up to a ventilator and a maze of other high-tech gadgets. The doctors want to press forward, insisting that there is a decent chance she may recover. Her nieces and nephews are not sure, however. Some feel there is no point in continuing all of this treatment, that Mabel wouldn't want any of it. Others are shocked by the suggestion of "letting go."

From the *Catechism:* Paragraphs 2258, 2276, 2288

These last three chapters are different from the first four. The preceding chapters discussed fundamental themes and basic faith convictions that serve as the foundation for the Christian moral life. We have seen that the Christian moral life is about responding to the amazing love of God. It is about participating in the work of the reign of God. And, as we strive to be people of good conscience, it is about the constant command and possibility that is ours to be converted from sin to the life of grace.

We now turn our attention to more specific questions, questions about what we are called to do or not do in specific areas of our life. In the present chapter, we focus on our responsibility to preserve our health and life as well as the health and lives of those entrusted to our care. In chapter 6, we examine important moral responsibilities in the area of human sexuality, and in the final chapter, we focus on some of our social responsibilities as followers of Christ. The fundamental themes and convictions examined in the first part of the book remain in place, of course, but the focus now is on what Christian moral life might look like in concrete situations.

So what really is best for Andrew in the tragic situation described above? How aggressive should the treatment plan be for this suffering eight-year-old boy? How shall Aunt Mabel's family proceed with the questions that face them? It seems that there is already some difference of opinion about the right thing to do on her behalf.

This chapter does not offer a recipe for simple solutions, but it does provide helpful wisdom from Catholic tradition, wisdom that is captured well in the *CCC*. We focus on long-standing Catholic teaching about the promotion of health and the preservation of life, convictions about "direct" and "indirect" killing, and some helpful criteria concerning the use and nonuse of medical treatment.

Catholic Convictions Concerning the Promotion of Health and the Preservation of Life

What kinds of responsibilities do we have to take care of our health and to preserve our lives? What kinds of responsibilities do we have to do the same for those entrusted to our care, that is, our children, our aging parents, and, if we are healthcare professionals, the patients we serve?

Over the centuries, Catholicism has been clear about the place to start in answering these questions.

> Human life is sacred because from its beginning
> it involves the creative action of God and it remains
> for ever in a special relationship with the Creator.
> *(Donum Vitae [Instruction on Respect for*
> *Human Life in Its Origins and on the*
> *Dignity of Procreation], introduction)*

> Life and physical health are precious gifts
> entrusted to us by God. We must take reasonable
> care of them, taking into account the needs of others and the common good. (*CCC*, #2288)

Two things in these passages are important to note. First, our attitude and readiness to act in regard to health and life are directly related to what might be called a Catholic "theology of creation." Life is sacred; it is a gift of the loving Creator. This is true of all that God has created, and it is particularly true of human life. Created in the image and likeness of God, and kept in existence by the provident hand of the Creator, every human being has a special relationship with God. God is the origin of our lives; God journeys with us in our lives here on earth, and eternal life with God is our final destiny. From beginning to end, life is sacred.

If this is true, then the implication for the families of little Andrew and Aunt Mabel in our opening stories is this: the decisions they face concerning an appropriate treatment plan for their loved one needs to begin with the faith-based conviction that human life is sacred. Human life is not only to be respected, but reverenced, especially when the human life is fragile, such as among the very young, the very old, or the very weak (see *CCC*, #2276). This latter idea is not one that the authors of the *CCC* made up on their own. It is a conviction that appears on nearly every page of the Bible and one that has been part of Christian tradition from the start: God is present in creation, in all human beings, but in a particularly dramatic way, God's abiding presence is with those who are suffering, with those who are vulnerable.

As we will see in chapter 7, in recent years Catholic teaching has emphasized that we should live our lives with a special "option for the poor," a particular love and concern for our brothers and sisters who are in need. This is also in order when medical-moral decisions must be made for persons like Andrew and Aunt Mabel. Their vulnerability stems not only from their physical condition, but also from their inability to speak for themselves and make their own decisions. They must rely on those who surround them to do what is genuinely in their best interests. When those who surround Andrew and Aunt Mabel do so with an awareness that in and through their "surrounding," God's care and compassion is being made manifest, then the decision-making process about what to do on their behalf is off to a good start.

But there is a second thing that we should note about the attitude Catholic tradition encourages in regard to the promotion of health and the preservation of life. Yes, we should be aware of the sacredness of life (our own and the lives of others), and yes, we should take reasonable steps to preserve the gifts of life and health (see *CCC*, #2288). But none of this means that we need to cling to our physical lives in some desperate way. Catholic tradition does not suggest that we take all measures at all times to prolong life. Life is sacred, but there may be times when other values and goods emerge as being even more important than the preservation of life. This is why we are able to honor martyrs (the most notable of whom was Jesus, of course)—those who have been willing to give up their lives rather than betray their faith. And it is the reason we honor as heroes and heroines those people who have given their lives in the service of their country, in the protection of innocent persons, or in some other noble and courageous manner.

Life is sacred, but at times other things may take precedence over the preservation of life. We are, after all, people who live with resurrection faith, with the conviction that death does not have the final say. When we "let go" and allow dying to run its course, rather than use medical treatments that would be inappropriately burdensome, it need not mean failure, either medically or spiritually. As we pray in the Eucharistic Prayer at Mass, Christians are those who believe that with death, life is changed, not ended.

Catholic Convictions Concerning Direct and "Indirect" Killing

So far, we have said that human life is sacred and that the basic attitude we should have toward life is one of reverence. This is the foundation of our responsibility to take reasonable steps to promote our health and preserve our lives as well the lives of those entrusted to our care. But we must be more specific. In this section, we examine a long-standing ethical norm within Catholicism concerning actions we should not take in regard to human life. In the next section, we discuss the principles the Catholic Church has proposed we use when faced with decisions about medical treatment.

Reflecting long-standing Catholic teaching, the *CCC* is clear in its teachings about euthanasia, suicide and assisted-suicide, and abortion.

> Whatever its motives and means, direct euthanasia consists in putting an end to the lives of handicapped, sick, or dying persons. It is morally unacceptable. (#2277)

And because "[w]e are stewards, not owners, of the life God has entrusted to us" (*CCC*, #2280), suicide "contradicts the natural inclination of the human person to preserve and perpetuate his life. It is gravely contrary to the just love of self" (#2281). Accordingly, assisting voluntarily in the suicide of another (whether one does so as a family member or in some "professional" capacity) is equally "contrary to the moral law" (*CCC*, #2282). Using the same categories and nearly identical language, the *CCC* also teaches that "Direct abortion, that is to say, abortion willed either as an end or a means, is gravely contrary to the moral law" (#2271).

These passages express a strong conviction: "the direct and voluntary killing of an innocent human being is always gravely immoral." These last words are from Pope John Paul II's encyclical letter *Evangelium Vitae (On the Value and Inviolability of Human Life*, #57), published in 1995. They are carefully chosen words, as are those in the *CCC*. Built into Catholic teaching here is a distinction between "direct" and "indirect" killing. What is absolutely forbidden—because it is contrary to what is humanly reasonable and, at the same time, contrary to the law of God (in Catholic teaching, the two can never conflict, and if they seem to, something is amiss)—is the "direct" killing of "innocent" human beings. An explanation of the words "direct" and "indirect" is obviously important.

There is a difference, Catholic tradition suggests, between "direct" and "indirect" killing. Taking the life of another "directly" comes about when one does something (or refrains from doing something) that is inevitably directed toward the death of a human being. "Direct" euthanasia (sometimes called "mercy killing") would take place if a physician were to give a patient a lethal dose of a drug in order to end the person's life so that he or she would no longer have to experience pain or suffering. Even if motivated by compassion, Catholic tradition judges this to be wrong because we do not have that kind of authority over the gift of life; we are "stewards," not "owners" of life. Similarly, in Catholic tradition, "direct" abortion comes about when, for whatever motives, an intervention is made that has as its goal the termination of the life of an unborn child. Why is this wrong? Because we are obliged to respect and protect human life from the moment of conception (see *CCC*, #2270).

Here we would do well to remember something from the discussion of conscience in chapter 3 and the treatment of what is required for someone to be guilty of sin, found in chapter 4. It is part of Catholic teaching that sometimes a person may do something that is "gravely wrong" objectively without necessarily being guilty of sinfulness personally. A variety of factors can diminish or even remove altogether one's degree of culpability or sinfulness "subjectively." In Catholic teaching, the action would still be considered "wrong"—perhaps seriously so, as is surely the case with the actions we discuss here—but no judgment would be made about the degree of sinfulness of the person involved.

So it is "direct" killing that Catholic teaching considers absolutely wrong. "Indirect" killing is another matter. Sometimes a person may do something (or refrain from doing something) that has both a primary, or "direct" effect (one that is good) and at the same time a secondary, or "indirect," effect (one that is regrettable and that would be avoided if it were possible to do so). As long as the person is "directly" intending ("aiming at") only the good effect, as long as the good effect is not brought about by the regrettable effect, and as long as there is a good enough reason to perform such an action in the first place, then performing this kind of action would be justified. If the action involves the loss of human life, Catholic tradition would call it "indirect" killing. Some examples should help.

It is "direct euthanasia" and it is wrong, Catholic teaching states, to give a lethal dose of a drug in order to end the life of a suffering patient. But it may be permitted and, indeed, be the objectively right thing to do to remove medical treatment that has become excessively burdensome or treatment that is no longer beneficial, even though one knows that doing so will most likely (even inevitably) lead to the death of the patient. A physician in an intensive care unit removes the ventilator from a patient who is in the end stages of cancer because the treatment is no longer beneficial. Or the family of little Andrew in our opening story decides not to proceed with further aggressive treatment, but simply to keep Andrew comfortable. Such decisions (in the first case "doing something," in the second case "refraining from doing something") are made with the awareness that the action or omission will most likely lead to the death of the patient. Even though it is foreseen, it is not the death of the patient that is directly "aimed at." What is aimed at is removing ineffective treatment or not initiating burdensome treatment. Yes, death may flow from such decisions, but in Catholic tradition, this is considered "indirect" killing and is justifiable. The same thing is at work in cases of legitimate self-defense. If persons need to use lethal force to protect themselves against unjust aggressors, long-standing Catholic teaching considers it to be justified because it is "indirect" or "unintentional" killing (see *CCC*, #2263).

In similar fashion, the *CCC* considers direct abortion to be gravely wrong, but it recognizes that interventions that involve "indirect" abortion may be justified. The most frequently used example is the case of a pregnant woman who is diagnosed with uterine cancer. Assuming that surgery cannot wait, an intervention to remove the cancerous uterus—resulting, regrettably, in the loss of the life of the unborn child as well as the loss of the woman's fertility—would be considered "indirect" abortion and would be justified. In a situation such as this, what is "directly" intended ("aimed at") is the good effect (preserving the woman's life); that good effect is not brought about by the regrettable effect (it is not the death of the unborn child that saves the woman's life); and, certainly, there is a good enough reason to perform such an action in the first place.

I hope you are not confused by all of this. Some of these ideas are difficult and some of these categories and distinctions are complex. But life is complex, and the more we attend to matters of detail, especially in situations in which life is at stake, the finer the instruments need to be to analyze them adequately. Indeed, there are some who think that the distinctions are needlessly complex and much more a matter of semantics than reality. It is not a surprise that those who are in favor of physician-assisted suicide (at least in some instances) and those who support the justifiability of euthanasia (in some cases) tend to say that the distinction between "direct" and "indirect" is a myth. "When the ICU physician removes the ventilator from a patient with end-stage cancer," these voices would suggest, "the physician is killing the patient. Let's just face up to it and look for the criteria for determining when it is right to kill someone and when it is not."

Catholic teaching is vehemently opposed to this stance, convinced that such a starting point will inevitably lead us to places we ought not go, places where the lives of vulnerable persons will be insufficiently protected and where reverence for life itself will be diminished. Catholic teaching argues that for all its complexity, the distinction between "direct" and "indirect" killing is not only real, but helps us draw a sharp line between right and wrong, a line that can help us be clear about what reverence for life can never allow.

Catholic Convictions Concerning the Use and Nonuse of Medical Treatment

We have looked at Catholic teaching that we must take reasonable steps to promote our health and preserve our lives and do the same for those entrusted to our care. We have also examined a long-standing (and strong) conviction that we should not do anything that would involve the direct termination of human life.

We now examine a different aspect of Catholic teaching regarding the care we are to take of our health and life.

No doubt, and fortunately, most of us are not interested in coming close to actions of euthanasia or assisted suicide—either for ourselves or for those entrusted to our care. But many questions remain. Just what kinds of medical treatments are we obliged to use to promote health and prolong life? For instance, what kind of medical treatment is appropriate for Andrew and Aunt Mabel in our opening stories? As the families of these vulnerable patients know, the answer to this question is not always obvious.

Catholic tradition does not offer a formula for simple solutions, but it does provide valuable wisdom. If the question is "What kind of medical treatment is appropriate to use in specific situations?" Catholic teaching answers, "It depends." Since the sixteenth century, theologians have suggested that we are obliged to use ordinary means of medical treatment, but we need not use extraordinary means to preserve health or life. Those categories have been described in various ways over the years, but in 1950, Catholic theologian Gerald Kelly offered these definitions:

> *Ordinary* means are all medicines, treatments and operations which offer a reasonable hope of benefit and which can be obtained and used without excessive expense, pain, or other inconvenience.

> *Extraordinary* means are all medicines, treatments, and operations which cannot be obtained or used without excessive expense, pain, or other inconvenience, or which, if used, would not offer a reasonable hope of benefit.
>
> ("The Duty to Preserve Life,"
Theological Studies, Vol. 12, 1950, p. 550)

This understanding of "ordinary" and "extraordinary" means of treatment, expressed here by a theologian, is what one finds in the writings of Pope Pius XII throughout the 1950s. And the substance of the same teaching was expressed in the *Declaration on Euthanasia* from the Vatican's Congregation for the Doctrine of the Faith in 1980. Though they are a bit long, the following passages from that declaration are important to examine.

> Is it necessary in all circumstances to have recourse to all possible remedies?. . . In the past, moralists replied that one is never obliged to use "extraordinary" means. . . . [Today] some people prefer to speak of "proportionate" and "disproportionate" means. In any case, it will be possible to make a correct judgment as to the means by studying the type of treatment to be used, its degree of complexity or risk, its cost and the possibilities of using it, and comparing these elements with the result that can be expected, taking into account the state of the sick person and his or her physical and moral resources. . . .

It is also permitted, with the patient's consent, to interrupt these means, where the results fall short of expectations. But for such a decision to be made, account will have to be taken of the reasonable wishes of the patient and the patient's family, and also of the advice of the doctors who are specially competent in the matter. The latter may in particular judge that the investment in instruments and personnel is disproportionate to the results foreseen; they may also judge that the techniques applied impose on the patient strain or suffering out of proportion with the benefits which he or she may gain from such techniques. (Sec. 4)

Note the kind of teaching the Church offers here. There are two criteria for determining whether an intervention is ordinary or extraordinary, whether it is ethically obligatory or not. First, does it offer a reasonable hope of benefit to this patient at this time? Second, can it be used without excessive expense, pain, or other burden?

Properly understood, the criteria defy a list of ordinary and extraordinary treatments. What is called for is a concrete judgment of what is right for this person in this time and place. And yes, sometimes even life-sustaining treatment may be forgone (either not initiated or removed if already in place) if the burden involved is disproportionate to the benefits that are likely to be gained. As we have discussed, if death were to result from a decision to forgo excessively burdensome or nonbeneficial treatment, Catholic teaching would consider it to be an instance of "indirect" killing.

The genius of this teaching is that it provides some criteria that are useful in all situations, and yet they are criteria that call for flexible applications in diverse situations. Sometimes chemotherapy, for example, may be judged appropriate because it offers a reasonable hope of benefit to a patient, and even though there is some real burden involved in the treatment, the patient judges that there is a proper proportion between the burdens and the hoped-for benefits. For another person (or later on in the course of the same person's disease), chemotherapy may be judged inappropriate because the proportion of burdens and benefits have become different. So, unlike the strong prohibition of all forms of euthanasia or "direct" killing, this teaching has a certain flexibility, one that recognizes the many different types of situations in which judgments about medical treatment need to be made.

Thus we should show our reverence for life by using treatments that seem to provide a reasonable hope of benefit and that are not excessively burdensome. But we need not be overzealous in doing so. To be sure, often death is not easy to embrace; "letting go" can require great courage. But our faith suggests that we need not cling to life desperately, as if life here is all there is. We are called to be grateful for the gift of life and to be good stewards of that gift, but we do well to remember that our life with God extends far beyond the horizon of this world.

For Reflection

1. What does it mean to you to say that human life is sacred? Can you identify a time in your life when you experienced the sacredness of human life? Try to describe that time. What are some of the things that can hinder our appreciation of the sacredness of human life? What are some things that can foster such an appreciation?

2. Do your best to explain in your own words the distinction between "direct" and "indirect" killing. Does this make sense to you? Are the examples in the chapter useful in helping you understand this distinction? Do they make sense to you? Why or why not?

3. The chapter does not discuss this directly, but the distinction between "direct" and "indirect" killing seems to indicate that there are some exceptions to "Thou shalt not kill." Note, however, that there are no exceptions to "Thou shalt not murder." What is the difference between "kill" and "murder"?

4. Catholic tradition suggests that when we are faced with decisions about medical treatment, we should apply the criteria of "burden" and "benefit." State in your own words what those criteria are. Do you find them helpful? Recall a time when you faced a decision about medical treatment and try to analyze that situation using the criteria of "burden" and "benefit."

FOR FURTHER READING

Ashley, Benedict M., OP, and Kevin D. O'Rourke, OP. *HealthCare Ethics: A Theological Analysis.* 4th ed. St. Louis: Catholic Health Association, 1989.

Congregation for the Doctrine of the Faith. *Declaration on Euthanasia.* New York: St. Paul Books and Media, 1980.

———. "Declaration on Procured Abortion," 1974.

———. *Donum Vitae (Instruction on Respect for Human Life in Its Origin and on the Dignity of Procreation),* 1987.

Connors, Russell B., Jr. "Decisions About Dying: A Moral Framework." *Church* 7, no. 4 (winter 1991): 18–22.

Kelly, David F. *Critical Care Ethics: Treatment Decision in American Hospitals.* New York: Sheed and Ward, 1991.

Shannon, Thomas A. *An Introduction to Bioethics.* 3rd ed. Mahwah, NJ: Paulist Press, 1997.

CHAPTER 6

Christian Morality and Human Sexuality

Father Williams

F ather Williams has a problem. It was hard enough knowing what to say to Lisa and Ron, and now Lisa's mom has
become involved.

Lisa and Ron approached Father Williams at the end of May
about getting married next summer. He enjoyed talking with them
when they met in June. They seemed mature and responsible and
fairly serious about their faith. So his initial response was that he'd
be delighted to help them prepare for their marriage, and he'd look
forward to celebrating their wedding with them. It was only at the
close of their conversation that an important issue arose.

The couple admitted that they were experiencing some "has-
sle" from Lisa's parents—especially her mom—about their decision to live together this coming year at the university (they
would be going back to school in a few weeks). Lisa's mom had
"exploded" over the idea; she was so upset she threatened to have
nothing to do with the wedding—perhaps she would not even
come—if the couple followed through on their plan.

"She's overreacting. She'll come around," Lisa said. "After all,
we've been going together since high school and our commitment to each other is very real. Besides, this isn't just about sex;
we are paying our own way at school, and living together is a lot
more realistic and practical economically." But Father Williams
knows Lisa's mother. And although he didn't acknowledge this to
Lisa and Ron, he agrees that she's a strong-willed person and can
be pretty difficult to deal with.

Father Williams felt good about the way he responded to the
couple. He talked with them about Catholic teaching on the subject, namely, that in the Church's eyes, sexual intercourse belongs
within the context of marriage. He spoke about a connection
between sexual intimacy and commitment, as well as the public
nature of their relationship. And he asked them to consider the
effect their decision might have on others, including their families. He didn't threaten them with a refusal to celebrate their
wedding unless they reconsidered, but simply asked them to give

their decision further thought. They said they would. Father Williams is planning to talk with them about this in August, just before they go back to school.

A call did come from Lisa's mom. "The family is scandalized by this," she insisted. "And frankly, Father, it doesn't seem like you've taken a very strong stand for what is right here, either!"

Father Williams agreed to meet with Lisa's mom. He's hoping the conversation will be helpful for everyone involved.

From the *Catechism:* Paragraphs 2331, 2332, 2337, 2347

Check your own experience on this. You are with a group of friends and the conversation suddenly takes a turn to something to do with sex. Does your interest level—and perhaps your level of discomfort—rise a bit? Does the tone of the conversation change? Is there a new kind of humor or perhaps a new kind of intensity? Do some people in the group speak more than others?

Whatever else we might say about sex, it is important. It may not be the most important part of life, but if the *CCC* is right, the things that human sexuality is about—affection, friendship, love, spirituality, and sometimes procreation—are far from trivial. Sometimes it is in regard to sexuality that we human beings are at our best. In these moments, sex can be about ecstasy and transcendence. But it is also the case, unfortunately, that we have been known to be at our worst when it comes to sexuality. In those moments, the experience of sexuality can be about exploitation and abuse.

Given all this, it is not surprising that Catholic tradition has paid great attention to this dimension of our lives, exemplified by the fact that the *CCC* discusses sexuality at some length. It does so first with some important reflections on sexuality itself and then with some specific moral norms related to sexual activity. In three sections, this chapter does the same. First, we examine some of Christianity's beliefs about creation and the goodness of sexuality, emphasizing, as does the *CCC*, the call to "integration," that is, the call to chastity. Second, we pay attention to the way Catholic teaching attempts to protect and promote important values at stake in sexuality through some of its specific moral norms. Specifically, we look at Catholic teaching about sex within marriage, about openness to procreation, and about homosexuality. We conclude with some brief comments about what the *CCC* calls "the laws of growth" in regard to sexuality. And, oh yes, along the way, we return to Fr. Williams' dilemma.

Christian Faith and Sexuality: Creation and Integration

The *CCC* begins its teaching about human sexuality with what might be called a "theology of creation." It does so by considering the great story of creation in the Book of Genesis, chapter 1 through chapter 2:4. We do not look to this story because we think it provides some sort of documentation of our origins. Rather, this story is a treasure because it reminds us of the sacredness of our origins. It invites our reflection on the fundamental goodness, indeed, holiness, of the gift of being sexual.

This first story of creation, referred to in the first paragraph in the *CCC* that discusses human sexuality, is the familiar legend that describes the seven "days" of creation. As creation gradually unfolds, we hear God's simple but powerful refrain that "it was good." The pinnacle of God's creative activity is reached when God decides, "Let us make humankind in our image, according to our likeness" (1:26). And the text continues: "So God created humankind in his image, in the image of God he created them; male and female he created them" (1:27).

In a twofold way, something of the nature—indeed, the mystery—of human sexuality is revealed here. First, we are not created in isolation from one another. We are not islands unto ourselves, designed in such a way that we must each pursue our own path to happiness and fulfillment. No, we are created with and for others. From the beginning to the end of our lives, we human beings are called to make our way in this world with one another. Living our lives in relationship with others is essential to who we are.

Second, notice that the story presumes that the creation of human beings as male and female not only is not a problem, but it is a grace. In our communion as men and women, we are the image of God. Sometimes Christian theologians have been tempted to see in this passage something of the doctrine of the Trinity—the doctrine of the communion of God as Father, Son, and Spirit. Surely, the human author of the story did not have in mind such a particular and precise way of thinking about God. Nevertheless, there is a hint here that God is not solitary. Created in God's image, neither are we solitary. Fashioned as male and female, we are different from one another, and that difference is meant to draw us together in a way that reflects nothing less than the holiness of God.

In chapter 3 of Genesis, we find another story that sheds further light on our origins and on the relationship of human beings to one another, particularly on what the relationship between men and women is meant to be. Symbolized by Adam and Eve, this is the story of humankind's "fall" from grace to sin. Prior to their sin, Adam and Eve related to one another—and to the rest of creation—in harmony. In one place, the *CCC* calls this "original justice": they were in right relationship with one another and with all other creatures (see *CCC*, #400). Naked in front of each other, they knew no shame.

After their rebellion against God, however, things changed. They realized their nakedness and sewed fig leaves together to cover themselves. And immediately, we begin to see tension and a lack of harmony between them; the man blames the woman for their misdeed, and she is told that henceforth her husband shall "rule over" her (Genesis 3:16). The *CCC* comments on this as follows:

> The harmony in which they had found themselves . . .
> is now destroyed: . . . the union of man and woman

becomes subject to tensions, their relations henceforth marked by lust and domination.[1]

The *CCC*'s insights here are important. They have, if you
will, a certain feminist tone to them. The relationship between
men and women should be marked by cooperation, harmony,
equality, and mutuality. The fact that so much of the history of
the relationship of men and women has been marked by tension
and domination—most often the domination of women by men
(what today we label patriarchy and sexism)—is nothing other
than a manifestation of human sinfulness. It has nothing to do
with the will of God, and it stands in need of personal and social
conversion.

Moving on from this theology of creation, the *CCC* discusses
at length what it describes as "The Vocation to Chastity" (see
#2337–2359). Let us reflect simply on what chastity is not, and
then describe what it is—more precisely, what it entails.

We begin with two important texts from the *CCC*.

> Chastity means the successful integration of sexual-
> ity within the person. . . . Sexuality, in which man's
> belonging to the bodily and biological world is
> expressed, becomes personal and truly human
> when it is integrated into the relationship of one
> person to another, in the complete and lifelong
> mutual gift of a man and a woman. (#2337)

> The chaste person maintains the integrity of the
> powers of life and love placed in him. This integri-
> ty ensures the unity of the person; it is opposed to
> any behavior that would impair it. It tolerates nei-
> ther a double life nor duplicity in speech.[2]

Three things are important in these passages. First, they make
clear what chastity is not. It is not some ill-fated and invariably
self-destructive attempt to deny or repress our sexual energies,
our need and longing for communion, intimacy, affection, and
love. As we have seen, nothing could be further from what
Catholic teaching considers the foundational truth about human

sexuality. We are created for relationship, for relationship with God and for relationship with one another (where we sometimes discover the presence of God). This is not just an idea. In our very bodies and emotions, we experience a desire for connection with others. Our faith invites us to believe that the desire itself has been placed within us by God. It is holy, and in some magnificent and mysterious way, reflects something of the nature of God. Chastity is the virtue that helps us express ourselves sexually in healthy and responsible ways. Denying this wonderful and important aspect of our lives is no virtue at all.

So chastity is not about denial or repression. What it is about, the *CCC* says, is integration. This is the second thing to note about the passages above. For the framers of the *CCC*, integration is an important concept, even if it is a little hard to define. Integration is about wholeness. Persons are integrated (this is really more like a goal than a "state") when they are living life in such a way that all the different aspects of their life fit together in a coherent and honest way. Integrated persons live with integrity. The way they live their life, the way they conduct themselves in various relationships and settings—at home and work, and with family, friends, fellow citizens, and their faith community—demonstrates a fundamental unity and consistency.

In regard to sexuality, chaste persons are sexually integrated persons. This means that in their relationships, they are able to express themselves in loving and affectionate ways, and in ways that are consistent with their commitments and state in life. Chastity or sexual integration, therefore, is expressed differently by different people. Praise God for the passionate ways in which chastity is expressed in the married couples who, after twenty years of marriage and four children, are still very much in love and continue to find their sexual intimacies both delightful and holy! Praise God for the single persons—single in many sets of circumstances—who are able to experience genuine intimacy in a number of important relationships in their lives, though perhaps sometimes with difficulty, and who are able to express and receive love and affection with both male and female friends!

Finally, let us not miss the brief comment made at the end of the second paragraph from the *CCC* quoted above: the chaste person's integrity "tolerates neither a double life nor duplicity in speech."[3] Chastity, or sexual integration, is the ability to express oneself sexually in ways that are honest. Presumed here, insightfully, I think, is the idea that in some ways, sexuality is like language. Language is to be used, not abused. To be able to speak, to be able to communicate, is one of the most amazing and wonderful things about being human. With language we are able to express who we are, and in some ways, to fashion who we are becoming. With language we can express love, make peace, communicate truth, and build bridges with other people.

Unfortunately, we do not always speak so well. Sometimes we express ourselves in ways that are dishonest and destructive. Chastity is the virtue that enables us to express ourselves sexually in ways that are not only affectionate and loving, but in ways that speak the truth about who we are.

Norms and Values: Specific Issues

It is time to examine several important norms of the Catholic Church regarding sexual activity. As we do so, it will become clear that these norms are meant to protect and promote key values that the Church considers essential to the moral meaning of human sexuality. So let us look at Catholic teaching about sex within marriage, openness to procreation, and homosexuality.

SEX WITHIN MARRIAGE

Catholic teaching insists that sexual intercourse belongs exclusively within the context of marriage. This is based on a conviction about what sexual intercourse means. In my mind this has never been said more positively than in *Humanae Vitae (On the Regulation of Birth)*, Pope Paul VI's encyclical letter of 1968 about birth control:

> Marriage is not, then, the effect of chance or the product of evolution or unconscious natural forces; it is the wise institution of the Creator to realize in humankind his design of love. By means of the reciprocal personal gift of self, proper and exclusive to them, husband and wife tend toward the communion of their beings in view of mutual personal perfection, to collaborate with God in the generation and education of new lives. (#8)

What is sexual intercourse about? Or, at least from a Catholic perspective, what is it meant to be about? It is meant to be the total gift of self to one's spouse. The totality and intimacy of the physical embrace, designed by the Creator to contribute to the mutual personal perfection of the spouses, is meant to be a sign— yes a sacrament—of the totality of the gift of self that the physical action displays. To say this differently, sexual intercourse seems to say "I give you all of me—bodily and spiritually," and that gift calls for the committed relationship of marriage. Moreover, as the *CCC* notes, the physical embrace of husband and wife should be a sign of their spiritual communion (see #2360).

I would add, their enduring spiritual communion. Thus the total gift of self that intercourse entails physically and spiritually ought not simply be a "moment" of physical or spiritual ecstasy, but rather a "gesture" that expresses and contributes to the enduring and committed love of the couple.

Perhaps this is what Father Williams did his best to explain to Lisa and Ron in our opening story. In his wisdom, Father Williams also seems to have tried to explain something about the public nature of their relationship, perhaps even the public nature of their sexual relationship. It would not be surprising if Lisa and Ron struggled with this latter idea. On the one hand, it is obvious that the sexual intimacy that intercourse entails has a decidedly private dimension to it. This is the way it should be. On the other hand, our culture tends to translate this into a proverb that goes something like this: "Whatever two consenting adults want to do sexually is their own private business."

Catholic teaching suggests that this attitude misses another important dimension of sexual intercourse. If it really is the total gift of self to another, and if it really is more than a momentary experience of intimacy and union, then in fact, it is an action that "calls for" the commitment of marriage. And that, of course, is a public matter. To say this in a different way, it is Catholic teaching that because of what sexual intercourse "says" ("I give you myself totally and in an enduring way"), when intercourse is "spoken" outside the context of marriage, it is not spoken with complete honesty. This is the case even for the sexual relations of those who are engaged (see #2350). It goes without saying that from the perspective of Catholic teaching, the sexual relations of those who are even further from a marital commitment—instances of "casual sex" and certainly prostitution—are even more seriously wrong.

OPENNESS TO PROCREATION

So it is Catholic teaching that sexual intercourse belongs within the context of marriage. That is not all. Inseparably linked to that teaching is the conviction that the sexual lovemaking of married couples must be marked by an openness to procreation. Marriage itself and sexual intercourse within the context of marriage are meant to be about love and life, and the two are essentially linked.

Two comments about this teaching are important. The first concerns the Church's insistence that it is not sufficient for the married couple's relationship to be open to procreation, or for their sexual activity, in an overall way, to be marked by such openness, but rather, "each and every marriage act must remain open to procreation." As is well known, this is the aspect of the teaching that has been most controversial and that has been difficult for many to understand or accept. According to Catholic teaching, there is something that is not right about a married couple taking deliberate steps—through the use of artificial means of contraception—to "cancel out" procreativity in a given act of intercourse. What this norm is attempting to protect and promote is the value of the inseparability of the unitive and pro-creative meanings of intercourse (see *CCC*, #2369).

Second, it is important to note that Catholic teaching does not say that couples may never take any measures to attempt to regulate the birth of children. What is inappropriate is the use of artificial means of contraception. However, if important factors make pregnancy at a given time inadvisable, couples are free to use natural means of regulating birth. That is, they are free to take account of the natural cycle of fertility and infertility of the woman in their pattern of lovemaking and, in that way, attempt to avoid pregnancy. (Note that attention to the same cycle of fertility and infertility can be used in an effort to achieve a pregnancy at a given time.)

In the Church's judgment, the use of artificial means of birth regulation is morally different from the use of natural methods. The wrongness of contraception stems from the way it involves "canceling out" procreativity in an act of intercourse. According to the *CCC*, it makes "the total gift of self" something less than total because one has taken a direct step to exclude a part of oneself, one's procreative potential, from that gift (see #2370). In contrast, natural means of birth regulation do not involve any direct steps to remove the procreative dimension from intercourse. Instead, they make use of the woman's cycle of fertility and infertility, and as Pope Paul VI taught, in that way they can be both natural and moral (see *Humanae Vitae*, #16).

Many couples report that these methods of birth regulation—even though they require discipline on the part of the couple—can be highly successful. In addition, they can promote a high degree of communication and cooperation between the spouses, sometimes leading to ever more creative ways of expressing love and even greater delight in sexual intercourse in their pattern of lovemaking.

HOMOSEXUALITY

The *CCC*'s discussion of homosexuality is brief—three paragraphs (see #2357–2359). Even so, the paragraphs capture the essence of Catholicism's convictions about those brothers and sisters who have a predominant and enduring sexual attraction (a sexual orientation) to members of their own sex. Three brief points are in order.

First, the *CCC* makes no moral judgment about homosexuality itself. As paragraph #2357 notes, the genesis of this sexual orientation (and probably the genesis of heterosexual orientation as well) is largely unexplained. As is well known, a variety of scientific disciplines—from genetics to biochemistry to medicine to psychiatry/psychology to anthropology—continue to study the genesis of homosexuality, but I think it can be said that the findings to date remain inconclusive. The *CCC* wisely acknowledges that, according to the experience of the men and women who describe themselves as "homosexual," this orientation is certainly not freely chosen (see #2358). Accordingly, there is no moral fault in the homosexual orientation itself. As stated in the Vatican's 1986 instruction "On the Pastoral Care of Homosexual Persons," the homosexual orientation is not a sin (see #3).

Second, if Catholic moral teaching does not focus on the homosexual orientation itself, it does focus on homosexual genital relations. As we have seen, Catholic tradition insists that sexual relations of such a physically intimate nature belong exclusively within the context of marriage. It is only in that context that they can be fully unitive and procreative—in an inseparable manner. As long-standing Catholic teaching has done, the *CCC* states that homosexual acts (that is, homosexual genital relations) are morally wrong both because such relations cannot be open to procreation and also because they are not marked by the interpersonal complementarity that genital relations are meant to display (see #2357).

Notice that the teaching is not that a homosexual couple may not be able to express their affection for each other in ways that are genuinely affectionate. The *CCC* insists that for all people the ability to express oneself in affectionate and loving ways in the important relationships of one's life is an important part of being human. But what the teaching is saying is that genital sexual relations belong within the context of marriage because of what those actions mean—the total gift of self, the gift of love and life inseparably.

Third, this teaching is difficult for many gay and lesbian persons, some of whom are members of our families and faith communities. Like all those who are not married, gay and lesbian persons are called to abstinence from genital sexual relations. (As we have noted, they are not called to isolation; they are not called to life without affection or love.) But unlike many unmarried persons, they cannot even look forward to a life that includes the kind of physical intimacy and lovemaking that married persons enjoy.

Catholic teaching in recent years has acknowledged this difficult dimension of the lives of those with a homosexual orientation. Accordingly, as the title of the Vatican document I referred to earlier indicates, gay and lesbian persons should be the recipients of a special form of pastoral care on the part of the Church and its ministers. They should receive the particular embrace and hospitality of the Christian community. And, above all, they should never be the recipients of any form of prejudice or discrimination—either in the Church or in society. As we know, unfortunately, that has not been the case. Gay and lesbian persons have far too often been the victims of not only discrimination, but hate crimes of all sorts, even murder. Even with its stance regarding homosexual activity, the attitude of the Catholic community toward gay and lesbian persons should be one of respect and welcome, with an eye to doing what we can to protect and promote their rights and well-being in both Church and society.

"Laws of Growth"

To many people both inside and outside of the Church, Catholic teaching has sometimes appeared to be bad news—more precisely, demanding, if not impossible, news. I am thinking here of some of the specific norms of the Church that we have just examined. Catholic teaching asks Lisa and Ron—very much in love and committed to each other—to wait until they are married to express their love in intercourse. Catholic teaching asks married couples to refrain from using artificial means of contraception, and, instead, to use natural methods of birth regulation, which include significant periods of time when they will need to refrain from intercourse and express their love in other ways. And Catholic teaching calls people with a homosexual orientation to abstain from genital sexual expression, to find other ways to express affection and love in the important relationships of their lives.

Over and above these specific examples, Catholic teaching calls us all to chastity, to sexual integration. Because we are human—not simply because we are Christians—we must strive to express ourselves in loving and affectionate ways, in ways that are consistent with our commitments and states of life, in ways that are marked by harmony and honesty.

All of this can be difficult. Even if one accepts the teachings of the Church on the matters listed above—and it is no secret that many conscientious Catholics struggle to grasp and accept some of these teachings—following these teachings can be difficult. And in regard to chastity, or "sexual integration," is this simply an ideal, perhaps an impossible one? Are we really able to live like this?

In an effort to be both compassionate and realistic, Catholic teaching responds with what the *CCC* calls "the laws of growth" (see #2343). Yes, we are called to "sexual integration," to chastity, and, yes, to a form of chastity that for all people at times, and for some people all the time, means abstinence from genital sexual intimacy and pleasure. This is where chastity directs us. But at any given time, what are we called to be and to do? We are called to be and to do the best we can—no more, no less. This, in my view, is what the *CCC* means by "the laws of growth."

To be clear, this does not mean that simply because we find chastity difficult at a particular time in our lives—as perhaps is the case for Lisa and Ron—then in those moments the moral law changes for us, so that we can do as we wish. No, chastity, or "sexual integration," as the *CCC* describes it, is the goal. It is what we ought to be aiming at—and God does not call us to what is impossible. And what is possible for us, concretely, at various places and stages on our life journey, is for each of us to determine concretely in our consciences, "the secret core and sanctuary of our lives." Sometimes what we are capable of in regard to chastity may be limited by all sorts of factors: by circumstances, age or level of moral development, maturity, ignorance, limitations on our freedom and, yes, sin. So, at any given time, we must simply do the best we can as we strive for "sexual integration," for chastity. None of us gets there easily, and perhaps none of us gets there completely. We need to strive to move on, but we also need to accept ourselves (and others) wherever we are on the journey.

A good pastor once told me that in regard to sexuality we should do three things: remember always that God loves us, refrain from judging others, and have a sense of humor about ourselves. He was a wise man.

ENDNOTES

1.   *CCC* 400: Cf. *Gen* 3:7–16.

2.   *CCC* 2338: Cf. *Mt* 5:37

3.   *CCC* 2338: Cf. *Mt* 5:37

For Reflection

1. This chapter suggests that in regard to sexuality we sometimes are at our best, but sometimes we can be at our worst. Does this seem right? If so, why?

2. Chastity, the *CCC* says, is about being "sexually integrated." What does this mean to you?

3. What should Fr. Williams say to Lisa and Ron? to Lisa's mother?

4. This chapter explains Catholic teaching about the connection between sexual intercourse and marriage, birth control, and homosexuality. Can you do the same? That is, can you explain these teachings in your own words? What are some of the values the Church seems to be trying to protect and promote through these teachings?

5. Recall the discussion about conscience in chapter 3: we should be guided by the Church's teachings as we make moral judgments, but the Church does not make them for us. We must act in accord with our conscience. How does this relate to Fr. Williams' "dilemma" with Lisa and Ron? Can it happen that, "in conscience," persons might judge that they must do something other than what the Church judges to be right and still be good Catholics?

6. What seems important about the notion of "laws of growth"?

For Further Reading

Cahill, Lisa Sowle. *Between the Sexes: Foundations for a Christian Ethics of Sexuality*. Philadelphia: Fortress Press, 1985.

Congregation for the Doctrine of the Faith. "Declaration on Certain Questions Concerning Sexual Ethics," 1975.

———. *Donum Vitae (Instruction on Respect for Human Life in Its Origin and on the Dignity of Procreation)*, 1987.

———. "On the Pastoral Care of Homosexual Persons," 1986.

Genovesi, Vincent J., SJ. *In Pursuit of Love: Catholic Morality and Human Sexuality*. Collegeville, MN: The Liturgical Press, 1987.

Molloy, Cathy. *Marriage: Theology & Reality*. Dublin: The Columbia Press, 1996.

Pope Paul VI. *Humanae Vitae (On the Regulation of Birth)*, 1968.

Whitehead, Evelyn Eaton, and James D. Whitehead. *A Sense of Sexuality: Christian Love and Intimacy*. New York: Doubleday, 1989.

CHAPTER 7

Christian Morality and Social Responsibility

LINDA

✦

I
t was quite a scene. Some were deeply moved; others
were not. The setting was a public hearing before a sub-
committee on welfare reform in the state senate.

Those who spoke to the senators were mostly women, a few
of whom (including Linda) had brought their children with
them. As the hearing proceeded, the children played with toy
blocks on the senate floor, a part of the scene not missed on the
evening news that day.

New workfare regulations had been set in place a few years
earlier. In recent months, sponsors of these workfare regulations
had boasted that large numbers of welfare recipients had moved
into the workforce, thereby receiving less in their welfare payments or perhaps no payments at all. "Our workfare initiatives
have been very successful," they reported. "This is not the time
to return to the handout policies of the past."

The senators heard a different side of the story from the
women, however. Many of them said that for them the new regulations had meant that they were no longer able to go to school
or participate in job-training programs. Instead, they had been
forced into minimum-wage jobs. Fighting back tears as she
spoke, Linda, a single mother of two children, recounted experiences ranging from anger to despondency. "The minimum-wage
jobs I have been forced to take are insufficient to support my
family," she insisted. "They usually come without health-care
benefits, and many of them do not hold out the possibility of
advancement. My children deserve better."

During a break in the hearing, one senator said to a colleague
that he thought it was good they were getting the perspective of
people like Linda, people whose lives had been affected by the
new workfare policies. But his colleague replied that he was angry.
"I feel manipulated by these well-coached women," he said. "We
can't return to the days of the free ride simply because of the emo-
tional stories of a few women. We must stay on course."

From the *Catechism:* Paragraphs 1881, 1905, 1906, 1930, 2448

Modern Catholic social teaching is commonly thought to have begun with the encyclical letter *Rerum Novarum (On the Condition of Workers)* of Pope Leo XIII in 1891. In that letter, the pope faced squarely the conditions of workers in what had become industrialized and urbanized Europe. In a word, the condition of many workers was miserable. Many workers, including children, worked long hours in sometimes horrific working conditions for shockingly small wages—nothing close to a wage that would support a family. In addition, housing and living conditions in the large industrial cities of Europe were equally miserable. Poverty was the condition of many.

What was somewhat new about the approach of Leo XIII in his letter of concern was that he did not simply call for a renewed effort at works of charity to assist those in need—although that was indeed part of his message. Much more forcefully, the pope called for justice. He called for a change in the social structures and institutions of the day that were the causes of the poverty and misery of the workers. He called for a just and living wage, for working conditions that were safe, and for laws that would prevent the abuse of children in the workforce. Fundamental to all of this was his insistence on the dignity of all people as children of God. He insisted that human dignity needs to be recognized and respected in the workers of the world.

Since Leo XIII, the Church has taken on the responsibility of addressing the issues of the day that concern the human community—sometimes matters of hunger and poverty, sometimes matters of prejudice and discrimination, sometimes matters of war and peace..Christian faith, popes and bishops have argued, should not lead us to try to escape these difficult problems, but to try to contribute to their solution in light of the Gospel of Christ. Over the last one hundred years, this has given rise to Catholic social teaching. Sadly, it is a body of teachings that has not received the attention it deserves, not even among Catholic people. As one of the books listed at the end of the chapter suggests, this gem of Catholic tradition may well be "our best kept secret."

In a variety of places, the *CCC* does its best to do justice to this wonderful tradition on justice. There are extensive sections, for example, that present the fundamental faith convictions that serve as a basis for Catholic social teaching. There are also several sections that address specific social justice issues. In this final chapter of the book, I do my best to present at least a taste of this important part of Catholic teaching.

The chapter consists of three parts. First, we look at some important faith convictions that ground Catholic teaching in this area, convictions about human dignity and human rights. Second, we look at the *CCC*'s teaching in regard to one important area of social concern: economic justice. We conclude with reflections on an important theme in Catholic social teaching: "preferential love for the poor."

Starting Points: Human Dignity and Human Rights

It has undoubtedly become clear that the Church's convictions about the dignity of the human person have a clear foundation in Christian faith. Our dignity as persons stems from the fact that we have been created in the image and likeness of God. Let us recall an image from one of the stories of creation in the Book of Genesis: "The Lord God formed man from the dust of the ground, and breathed into his nostrils the breath of life; and the man became a living being" (Genesis 2:7).

What a wonderful image: we have been created by the life-breath of God. Nothing less than the breath of God animates us. In the New Testament, the same image is used to describe Christ's gift of the Spirit to the disciples after the Resurrection. John's Gospel reads as follows: "'Peace be with you. As the Father has sent me, so I send you.' When he had said this, he breathed on them and said to them, 'Receive the Holy Spirit'" (20:21–22).

Again, what a marvelous image, and what a powerful way to ground our convictions about the dignity of human persons. Created by the life-breath of God, and animated by the Spirit of God—whom Christians believe to be present not only in followers of Christ, but in all people of good will—we are all dwelling places of the life and holiness of God. As the U.S. Catholic bishops wrote in their letter about war and peace in 1983 ("The Challenge of Peace: God's Promise and Our Response," included in O'Brien and Shannon, *Catholic Social Thought*): "The human person is the clearest reflection of God's presence in the world. . . ." (#15). People are holy, Catholic tradition states. This is the source of our dignity, a dignity that calls for not only respect, but through the lens of faith, reverence.

Flowing directly from the dignity of the human person, Catholic tradition calls for the recognition of and respect for fundamental human rights. Catholic teaching insists that human rights are not conferred upon individuals because they are citizens of a given society. No, the origin of human rights is found in the nature of the human person as such; they are neither given nor (legitimately, at least) taken away by society. Society exists to protect and promote the dignity and rights of people, not the other way around.

What exactly do we mean by "rights," and what are some examples? The *CCC* does not provide a definition of human rights. In fact, the concept is difficult to define. But drawing on the insights of theologian J. Milburn Thompson (see bibliography), we can affirm that the dignity of the human person, realized in community, is the foundation of a Catholic approach to human rights. And flowing from this, it can be said that human rights are those basic human goods that are due to human beings so that they can develop themselves fully as persons living in community.

Some like to think of human rights as the minimum that we have "coming to us" simply because we are human beings. Protection and promotion of human rights are important not simply so that we can survive or "get by" in life, but so that we can strive to flourish as human persons. Isn't that what Linda in our opening story seems to be looking for? Doesn't she want more for herself and her children than "getting by"? Catholic teaching suggests that Linda's desire for more than that is part of what human dignity is all about.

It is important to flesh out Catholicism's view of human rights with some examples. As we will see in the next section when we focus on economic justice, the *CCC* discusses some of the rights of persons in specific arenas of life. But to move beyond the *CCC* for a moment, it is commonly acknowledged that the most complete list of human rights in Catholic social teaching is found in Pope John XXIII's encyclical letter of 1963, *Pacem in Terris (Peace on Earth)*. It is worth seeing at least part of the pope's list. According to Pope John XXIII, human rights include:

- The right to life and a worthy standard of living: the right to bodily integrity, food, clothing, shelter, healthcare, and necessary social services (#11)

- Rights pertaining to moral and cultural values: the right to one's good reputation, to search for truth, to be informed about public matters of concern, etc. (#12–13)

- The right to worship God according to one's conscience (#14)

- The right to choose one's state in life (#15–17)

- Economic rights: a right to work, to work in a safe environment, and to receive a just wage; also a right to private property (and other sources of wealth) as long as this does not interfere with more basic rights of others (#18–22)

- The right to meet and associate with others (#23–24)

- The right to emigrate and immigrate: especially necessary given the injustices and oppression that exist in some places and countries (#25)

- Political rights: one's ability to take an active part in the civil and political life of one's community (#26)

Obviously, a lot of detail is left for interpretation and application—such as what one means by "necessary social services," or what exactly a right to health care includes. In our own country, for example, it would not be hard to imagine both Democrats and Republicans espousing this list of human rights but disagreeing on how minimally or maximally the government should become involved in seeing to it that they are secured. Even so, by any standard, this exposition of human rights sets an agenda for what every society should be concerned about. Catholic social teaching insists that flowing from human dignity, human rights are important so that we can strive to develop ourselves fully as human beings, in keeping with our common vocation to live as creatures fashioned in the image of God (see *CCC*, #1877).

A final comment about human rights is important. If emphasis on human rights is the right hand of Catholic social teaching, emphasis on the common good is the left hand. The good of individuals and the good of the community are essentially connected (see #1905). The good of individuals cannot rightly be promoted at the expense of the common good, and the common good should never be promoted at the expense of the good of individual persons. A society is well ordered when the two are held in balance.

This balance is explained well in the following paragraph of the *CCC*, in which a definition of the common good is provided.

> By common good is to be understood "the sum total of social conditions which allow people, either as groups or as individuals, to reach their fulfillment more fully and more easily." The common good concerns the life of all. It calls for prudence from each, and even more from those who exercise the office of authority. (#1906)

Two things about this paragraph are important. First, noting how the paragraph ends, concern for the common good needs to be a special concern for those in positions of authority and leadership. Legislators, governors, and civic officials must be attentive to the needs of individuals—individual groups within the community as well as individual persons—but they are particularly charged to oversee the common good. That is, it is especially their responsibility to see to it that the laws and policies of the community contribute to the order and harmony of the community as such. They must see to it that all are receiving their fair share of the community's goods and resources (health care, access to education, police protection, etc.), and at the same time are contributing their fair share to the common good (through the paying of taxes, military service, etc.). Note that "fair share" need not mean mathematical equality. Thus, the health care resources that someone "consumes" (in some ways at the community's expense) are based not on an abstract formula that ensures mathematical equality but rather on need. And in a similar way, the "fair share" that one contributes to the common good (especially through income taxes) takes into account, appropriately, one's resources and capacity to contribute. As these examples illustrate, oversight for the common good by those in authority is tricky and controversial. Perhaps in some ways the common good is an ideal that the community continually strives for; promoting it is as much an art as a science.

The second thing to note in the paragraph above is that the common good is not simply a matter of concern for people in authority. Rather, it "concerns the life of all." This is made evident in the section of the *CCC* that immediately follows the discussion of the common good (see #1913–1917). Those paragraphs are about responsibility and participation. They describe how it is the responsibility of all persons to promote the common good (see #1913). So it is not sufficient to make decisions—in one's business affairs or in the way one votes, for example—simply on the basis of self-interest or the interests of individual good. No, Catholic tradition would insist, we are each charged to some degree with concern for the common good, with doing not only what will serve our own interests, but what will serve and benefit others as well, particularly those in need. It would be too simple—and unrealistic—to place the burden of the common good solely in the hands of our leaders. As the term suggests, the common good must be the concern of all of us.

This emphasis on the common good serves as an important balance to Catholic tradition's emphasis on human rights. The way John XXIII put it years ago in *Pacem in Terris*, rights and responsibilities go together. That is why he followed his list of human rights with a similar list of duties and responsibilities that we all have as members of society (see #28–38). A society driven solely by individual self-interest necessarily makes us all competitors. We are more than that, Catholic social teaching suggests. We are sisters and brothers. We must be collaborators with one another by helping to fashion a just society, and in that way, helping to fashion God's reign of justice, love, and peace.

Focus: Economic Justice

The *CCC* has quite a lot to say about economic justice. This is not surprising, since virtually every pope from Leo XIII at the turn of the last century to John Paul II in our own day has written and spoken often about justice in this arena of life. The *CCC* represents this well, and in the paragraphs that follow we try to do the same as we examine some of the things the *CCC* says about economic justice.

The Church's primary conviction about economic justice is stated clearly as follows:

> The development of economic activity and growth in production are meant to provide for the needs of human beings. Economic life is not meant solely to multiply goods produced and increase profit or power; it is ordered first of all to the service of persons, of the whole man, and of the entire human community. (#2426)

These two simple sentences pose a set of enormously challenging questions: What is it that drives the economic decisions of individuals, corporations, and countries? Is it purely and simply the drive for power, for profit? Is this the only thing that we find on "the bottom line"? If so, Catholic social teaching suggests, something is fundamentally wrong. Catholic teaching suggests that what should drive all economic decisions is not simply a desire for profit but, more fundamentally, the well-being of persons and the human community. This, the *CCC* says, should be the "moral bottom line." This does not mean that seeking to make a profit in one's business transactions is, by definition, morally wrong. But it does mean that from a moral point of view the standard of economic success needs to be more than the gross national product; it needs to be deeper than dollars and cents. What are our economic decisions and policies doing to and for people? Catholic social teaching suggests that this question must be "factored in" to what economic success means.

Is this a challenging question? Of course it is. But it is a question that we should all be trying to keep before us in the economic decisions we make as individuals, families, corporations, and nations. To return to the story that introduced this chapter, for example, if one were interested in assessing the success of new workfare programs and policies around the nation, Catholic teaching suggests that the assessment criteria must include what those policies have done to and for people, people like Linda. From a moral point of view, it is not enough to focus on only the tax dollars those policies may have saved. For individuals and institutions, something more is required.

It is worth noting that the U. S. Catholic bishops have acknowledged that the Church's principles about economic justice should be applied to the Church itself. The Church, after all, is an economic actor as a consumer, owner, employer, and investor (see "Economic Justice for All", #347–358, found in O'Brien and Shannon, *Catholic Social Thought*). Do the Church's institutions keep this question before themselves sufficiently in their own decisions and policies? No, they do not, as the bishops acknowledged. Without letting anyone "off the hook," and without trying to "water down" the question posed by Catholic teaching, it does seem true that the question suggests a goal, an ideal, more than specific economic policies. Perhaps what all economic actors—large and small—should be looking for is the degree of progress that is being made in seeing to it that our "bottom line" is measured not simply by what we have earned, but by what we have done to and for people.

The *CCC* moves from this fundamental conviction to address several other, more specific, areas of economic concern. Let us do the same by examining the *CCC*'s teaching about human work and the role of the state in economic affairs.

Consistent with the fundamental starting point that we have just examined, the *CCC* looks at work not simply from the perspective of what workers do, but what work does to and for workers. Drawing from the writings of Pope John Paul II, who has written much about this in his social encyclicals, the *CCC* offers important insights about the nature of human work.

Work is obviously important because many of us spend a high percentage of our lives at our work, and because it is essential for our livelihood. But the *CCC* suggests something more. It emphasizes that it is through work that we fulfill a part of our human nature. Work is one of the ways we develop ourselves as persons (see #2428). It is through our work that we are able to express ourselves, fulfill ourselves, and contribute to the human community. These ideas may strike some of us as unrealistic—ideals that are a long way from reality. Sadly, that is the case for too many people. For many, work is routine, burdensome, even oppressive. Catholic social teaching argues that this is not as it should be. Workers ought to be given an opportunity to take responsibility for what they do, to make their work their own. The more this happens, Catholic social teaching argues, the more work can become an opportunity for self-expression, for personal fulfillment, and for the satisfaction that comes from making a genuine contribution, even if a small one, to the well-being of other people. Put differently, if work is for people, and not the other way around, then those responsible for the work that other people do should be looking for ways in which that work can both express and promote human dignity.

In addition to these goals regarding human work, the *CCC* also names several more concrete things that relate to justice for workers. First of all, men and women should have access to employment in ways that are fair. The professions and the workforce should be "open to all without unjust discrimination . . ." (#2433). Second, workers should receive a just wage for the work they do. This means a wage that allows one to provide a reasonable and dignified quality of life for oneself and one's family materially, socially, culturally, and spiritually (see #2434). The *CCC* notes that it is not morally sufficient that a contract has been reached between employers and workers. A just wage must meet more stringent criteria; it must take into account the quality of life it allows a person and his or her family to enjoy (see #2434). Third, workers should have recourse to a strike when it becomes morally legitimate (see #2435). Reasons that might warrant such a strike (which should always be carried out in nonviolent ways) include not only unjust wages but also unsafe or burdensome working conditions. As we have seen, the dignity and rights of persons call for safe working environments. Finally, the *CCC* notes that workers have a right to social security contributions that (in countries like our own) are required by legitimate authority (see #2436). The *CCC* does not include health care benefits with this, largely because in many countries health care is provided by the state and not linked to employment. But in countries where access to health care (which Pope John XXIII listed as a human right) is linked to employment, an argument could surely be made from Catholic teaching that employers should be required to see to it that their workers are provided with health care benefits. In exchange for all of this, workers have serious obligations to fulfill their own responsibilities to their employers with honesty and integrity. Although it seems accurate to say that the *CCC*'s emphasis is clearly on the rights of workers, it is also true, as we have noted, that rights and responsibilities go together.

We conclude this section by noting what the *CCC* says about the responsibility of the state in regard to economic justice. In paragraph #2431, the *CCC* discusses the important role the state has in providing a sense of stability and security economically. Providing "a stable currency and efficient public services" are two things the state can do to establish and maintain such stability and security. However, as far as guaranteeing the protection of human rights (especially economic rights) is concerned, the *CCC* is insightful and clear in declaring that it is not only the state that "owns" this responsibility; it belongs to all of us (see #2431).

Catholic social teaching tries hard to avoid espousing a particular form of government as the normative way in which economic life should be ordered and human rights protected. Sometimes, because of Catholicism's strong emphasis on human rights—rights that according to Pope John XXIII include not only food, clothing, shelter, and rest, but medical care and necessary social services—it has seemed to many that Catholic social teaching is virtually an espousal of "big government," indeed, even socialism. In fact, Catholic tradition intends to steer clear of espousing a particular political party or a specific style of government. That is why the *CCC* emphasizes that it is not the exclusive role of the state to see to it that human rights, especially economic rights, are recognized and respected. The primary responsibility for the protection and promotion of human rights lies with all of us, both as individuals and as members of institutions.

In discussions about policies and programs in the economic arena (arguments about job-training programs like the ones no longer available to Linda, for example) we often hear some insist that the government needs to exercise greater responsibility, while others argue that "the private sector" can more effectively deliver what people need. Catholic teaching suggests that it is a matter of both-and, not either-or. To paraphrase a passage from the Book of Genesis (see 4:9), if we ask "Who is my brother's and my sister's keeper?" Catholic social teaching answers "All of us."

"Preferential Love for the Poor"

This chapter concludes with some reflections on an important theme in Catholic tradition: our call to have "a preferential love for the poor." To be sure, this key element of Catholic social teaching has important implications for how we live our lives individually and together. But really it is larger than that. First and foremost, the phrase "preferential love for the poor" says something about God; second, it says something about us. The paragraphs that follow reiterate some of the things we said about God in chapters 1 and 2, and connect these things with what they mean for us, what they mean for us as followers of Christ.

The first two chapters of this book, like two sides of a coin, suggest that reflection on the nature of the Christian moral life should begin with reflection on God. Chapter 1 focuses on the unconditional, unfathomable gift of God's love for us. God loves us not because of what we have done, but because of who we are—God's creatures. It can't be otherwise, for God is love. The Christian moral life begins with the recognition of this gift, and it becomes the desire and lifelong "project" of Christians to try to find appropriate ways to respond to God's love, to "act it out" in the ways we treat other people.

Chapter 2 focuses on the biblical image of the reign of God. We begin by reflecting on the centrally important story in the Book of Exodus about the way God heard the enslaved Israelites' cries of affliction and "came down" to act on their behalf. In and through Moses, God led the Israelites from slavery to freedom. This story, we conclude, reveals something important about God: yes, God loves all people, God cares about everyone, but God seems to have a particular love and care for those who suffer. Moreover, if the Christian story—the story about Jesus Christ—reveals anything, it reveals the extent to which God will go in caring for the weak and wounded of the world: in Jesus, God identified with the poor and the powerless. He became one of them, and in solidarity with all those who ever have suffered or would suffer, he went to his death with faith and integrity, only to be raised up victorious over death. Because of the resurrection of Christ, Christians find the faith and hope to believe that the reign of God that Jesus preached—a reign of justice, love, and peace—is not an illusion, but that it is at hand. In light of this, the Christian moral life can be described as the effort to participate in God's work of fashioning a reign of justice, love, and peace.

So what does the phrase "preferential love for the poor" refer to? It refers to God's love. It refers to God's way of being and acting toward those who are poor or needy in any way. To be clear, it does not mean that God loves some people more than others. God's love is universal; it extends to all the cracks and corners of God's creation, and especially to the cracks and corners of the wounds of individual persons.

As we have seen, all analogies fall short—certainly those about God. But perhaps the preferential love of God for the poor can be compared to the way in which the love of a parent becomes focused on the child who is hurting, the child whose needs call for a particular manifestation of parental love and compassion. Isn't this part of the message of the story in Luke's Gospel about the forgiving father and the prodigal son (see 15:11–32)? The father loved both sons, but the neediness of the prodigal son upon his return called for the special love and embrace of the father. So it is with God. God loves all people, but God has a preferential kind of love for those who are poor and suffering.

It will come as no surprise where this reflection about God's preferential love of the poor leads us. We are back to the idea we have seen in the First Letter of John, "Beloved, since God loved us so much, we also ought to love one another" (4:11). How should we love one another? In the same way God loves us. And just as God's love is directed in a particular way toward those who are in need, our love must be similarly directed. So if a "preferential love for the poor" describes God's way of becoming involved in this world, the same should be true for us (see *CCC*, #2448).

We can conclude with three comments about this theme. First, a preferential love for the poor is not first and foremost a program. It is an attitude, one that springs from a grateful heart. And who among us might be most inclined to have such an attitude? Those, I think, who have at some point in their lives been on the receiving end of the gracious and compassionate love of God, probably through the gracious and compassionate love of others. Consult your own experience. Those whose experience has taught them that love is not really "merited," but rather that genuine love (surely the love of God) is always a gift, are most likely to be the ones who know that this is the kind of love that is most Godlike, the kind of love worth spending a lifetime trying to manifest to others.

Second, if it is true that a preferential love for the poor is not first of all a program, it is equally true that sometimes it needs to become one. Put differently, a preferential love for the poor is not simply an idea or a feeling. If it is real it must be made manifest in concrete deeds and actions—sometimes daring and costly ones—on behalf of our needy neighbors. Just as in the story from the Book of Exodus God "came down" to take the side of the Israelites in their slavery and oppression, so too a preferential love for the poor must "come down" from our heads and show itself in our hands. If it begins in the heart it does not end there. It must show itself in actions—both individually and collectively.

So, yes, sometimes a preferential love for the poor can and does show itself in the policies and practices of communities and institutions. I am thinking, for example, of a Catholic hospital in a poor neighborhood of a large city (fortunately, there are many Catholic hospitals like this) that factors into its budget the several million dollars it will spend every year providing health care to those who do not have health insurance and are not likely to be able to pay for it themselves. That is how this hospital does things. It displays a "preferential love for the poor" in its way of doing business.

Finally, to recall one of our reflections about conversion in chapter 4, our call to have a preferential love for the poor is not only a command, but a possibility. Like many of the things this book has said about the Christian moral life, living our lives with a preferential love for the poor is difficult. Loving others as God has loved us is difficult. And contributing to the work of justice, love, and peace—and in that way helping to fashion the reign of God—may be so costly at times that it comes to resemble nothing less than the cross of Christ.

But the command is also a possibility, one that can bring immense joy and peace. The example of the hospital in the paragraph above makes this clear. The sisters who sponsor and "run" this hospital—against the odds—do so with immense pride and satisfaction. Manifesting the best of Catholic faith, and displaying the best of Catholic convictions about social responsibility, they speak about their work with pride and humility. They speak of their faith conviction that the Spirit of God has been with them all along in their work and that the Spirit remains with them today in their commitment to care for their needy neighbors. The Spirit of God, they remind us, enables them to be and do far more than they might have imagined.

❧✠❧

FOR REFLECTION

1. What are the implications for you of saying, as the U.S. Catholic bishops have said, "The human person is the clearest reflection of God's presence in the world?"

2. What are your responses to the summary of Pope John XXIII's list of human rights given in this chapter? Is this kind of list important? realistic? idealistic? Would you make any additions or deletions to the list?

3. The chapter argues that rights and responsibilities belong together, as do our concerns for one's individual good and the common good. Do you agree? If you do, give some examples that demonstrate the connection between rights and responsibilities.

4. Catholic social teaching suggests that as we face economic decisions, "the bottom line" should include concern for people as well as profit. Can you give examples of people and businesses that seem to try to make economic decisions on this basis?

5. What does "preferential love of the poor" mean to you? What does it not mean?

FOR FURTHER READING

Coleman, John A., SJ, ed. *One Hundred Years of Catholic Social Thought: Celebration and Challenge.* Maryknoll, NY: Orbis Books, 1991.

Door, Donal. *Option for the Poor: A Hundred Years of Catholic Social Teaching.* Maryknoll, NY: Orbis Books, 1992.

Henriot, Peter J. et. al. *Catholic Social Teaching: Our Best Kept Secret.* Maryknoll, NY: Orbis Books, 1988.

O'Brien, David J., and Thomas A. Shannon. *Catholic Social Thought: The Documentary Heritage.* Maryknoll, NY: Orbis Books, 1992.

Thompson, J. Milburn. *Justice & Peace: A Christian Primer.* Maryknoll, NY: Orbis Books, 1997.

Conclusion

This little book began by acknowledging that Christian morality is often considered to be "the dark side of the Good News." It can appear to some to be all about rules and regulations or about impossible ideals (like being told that we are to forgive others in the same way that God has forgiven us) that leave some of us feeling "we just can't do it."

If these pages have come even close to accomplishing their purpose, it should be clear that there is another side of the story. The Christian moral life may be difficult, but it is not "the dark side of the Good News." Serious obligations (both personal and communal) and challenging ideals are indeed part of the package of following Christ, but they are not the heart of the matter. To invoke a biblical image used in several of the preceding chapters, Christian morality is, at its heart, living "in the breath of God."

The author of the second story of creation from the book of Genesis described the creation of humankind this way: "The Lord God formed man out of the dust of the ground, and breathed into his nostrils the breath of life; and the man became a living being" (Genesis 2:7). And in the Gospel of John, when Jesus appears after the Resurrection to the disciples—the disciples who were paralyzed by some combination of confusion, fear, and guilt—his first words to them are "Peace be with you" (John 20:19). And then we read, "'As the Father has sent me, so I send you.' And when he had said this, he breathed on them and said to them, 'Receive the Holy Spirit'" (John 20:21–22).

The Genesis passage invites us to believe that we have been created by the gift of the breath of God, and that God continues to breathe in us and in all of creation, especially in all human beings. From this point of view, the moral life is nothing other than an invitation to recognize and reverence the gift of God's life, God's breath, in ourselves and in all we meet. The passage from John invites followers of Christ to believe that the risen Christ continues to offer us peace and continues to breathe the Holy Spirit of God into our hearts. And just as the breath of the Spirit of God transformed the disciples, unleashing in them energy for proclamation, for healing, for reconciling, for peace making, and for justice building (all of which they would have thought to be far beyond their capabilities), so too, the breath of the Spirit of God in us is our source of energy for the same work of building up the reign of God. The Christian moral life, these passages suggest, is not first and foremost about what we do; it is about what we are willing to let God do in us and through us.

BIBLIOGRAPHY

Catechism of the Catholic Church. Washington, DC: United States Catholic Conference, 1994.

Congregation for the Doctrine of the Faith. "Declaration on Ethanasia," 1980.

————. *Donum Vitae (Instruction on Respect for Human Life in Its Origins and on the Dignity of Procreation)*, 1987.

————. "On the Pastoral Care of Homosexual Persons," 1986.

Kelly, Gerald. "The Duty to Preserve Life." *Theological Studies* 12 (1950): 550.

National Conference of Catholic Bishops. *The Challenge of Peace: God's Promise and Our Response.* Washington, DC: United States Catholic Conference, Inc., 1983.

O'Brien, David J., and Thomas A. Shannon. *Catholic Social Thought: The Documentary Heritage.* Maryknoll, NY: Orbis Books, 1992.

Pope John XXIII. *Pacem in Terris (Peace on Earth)*, 1963.

Pope John Paul II. *Dominum et Vivificantem (Lord and Giver of Life)*, 1986.

————. *Evangelium Vitae (On the Value and Inviolability of Human Life)*, 1995.

Pope Leo XIII. *Rerum Novarum (On the Condition of Workers)*, 1891.

Pope Paul VI. *Humanae Vitae (On the Regulation of Birth)*, 1968.

Second Vatican Council. *Gaudium et Spes (Pastoral Constitution on the Church in the Modern World)*, 1965.

Thompson, J. Milburn. *Justice & Peace: A Christian Primer.* Maryknoll, NY: Orbis Books, 1997.

Acknowledgments

About the Author

Russell B. Connors Jr., Ph.D., a native Clevelander, studied Christian ethics at the Academia Alfonsiana in Rome, Italy, where he earned a doctoral degree in 1983. He served on the faculty of St. Mary Seminary in Cleveland from 1983 to 1995 and now teaches at the College of St. Catherine in St. Paul, Minnesota. Dr. Connors was the 1990–91 Fellow in Bioethics at the National Institutes of Health in Bethesda, Maryland, and has served as a consultant to the ethics committees of several hospitals and nursing homes. He has published numerous articles on Christian ethics in a variety of scholarly journals, and with Patrick T. McCormick (Gonzaga University), he is co-author of *Character, Choices, and Community: The Three Faces of Christian Ethics,* published by Paulist Press..